Business Communication

Bestoon Abdulmaged Othman

Dr. Preeti Chitkara

Dr. Sulabh Chitkara

Dr Deepa C Devaraj

Published By: BR International

Website: https://www.brinternational.net/

Email: Publish@brinternational.net

Mobile: +91-9695375469

1ST Edition: -2024

ISBN: 978-81-965444-2-3

Content

Content — **Page No**

Unit- I — 1

Business Communication – Introduction, Communication, And Organization Structure

Chapter 1: Business Communication–Introduction — 1 - 13

Chapter 2: Communication And Organization Structure — 14 - 40

Unit- II — 41

Organizations And Communication In The Context

Chapter 1: Culture And Communication Within The Organization — 41 - 46

Chapter 2: Communication And Technology — 47 - 56

Chapter 3: Information And Communication Technology — 57 - 69

Unit- III — 70

Correspondence On Recruitment

Chapter 1: Employment Applications And Resume Development — 70 - 87

Chapter 2: Employment Interviews And Correspondences — 88 - 106

Unit- IV — 107

Oral And Written Communication In Organizations

Chapter 1: Oral Communication — 107 - 124

Chapter 2: Written Communication   125 - 143

Unit- V Business Letters And Report Formulation   **144**

Chapter 1: Business Letters   144 - 157

Chapter 2: Memorandum And Report Writing   158 - 169

Chapter 3: Employing The Case Study Approach   170 - 182

Unit- VI Presentation Skills And Communication   **183**

Chapter 1: Presentation Skill   183 - 195

Chapter 2: Group Communication   196 - 217

Bibliography   218 - 223

Preface

Individuals in businesses invest a lot of time communicating with one another. For instance, scientific studies consistently show that managers invest more than 60% of their overall time in meetings. In certain circumstances, people invest more than 80% of their day communicating. As a result, communication is among the fundamental aspects of administration in any business, and its significance cannot be overstated. It is the act of passing facts, concepts, thoughts, views, and initiatives from one component of a company to another. In addition to being effective communication essential for good human relationships, it is also needed for a productive and profitable business. Competent information and decision-making communication are critical components of management-worker relationships.

One can communicate verbally or in writing. In written communication, the content in the statement is a mirror of our ideas as opposed to oral communication, when audiences can understand what the individual is trying to communicate. To prevent their content from being misunderstood, written communication or statements ought to be precise, obvious, and short. Written communication enables employees the chance to submit their thoughts in writing and offers a persistent document for utilization in the future. So, for a business to function well, efficient communication is crucial. The goal of this book is to demonstrate both the difficulty of business communication and its potential for improvement.

Unit-I

Business Communication – Introduction, Communication, And Organization Structure

Chapter- 1

Business Communication–Introduction

Introduction

The Latin term "Communis" which implies to transmit, engage in, distribute, or create commonplace is the source of the English word "communication." It is a procedure where evidence, concepts, and views are exchanged for a person or company to express meaning and comprehend each other. Across other aspects, it involves interaction and communication of information comprising realities, beliefs, opinions, feelings, and mindsets. The advancement of humanity has indeed been facilitated by the capacity to interact between frontiers and all over cultures. The capacity to facilitate quick and efficient communications across borders is what has lowered distances and brought "global capitalism" into being. Communication seemed to be necessary to ensure that members of one nation, civilization, or linguist community interacted and related with members of certain other nations, civilizations, or linguist communities. Life on this earth acquires relevance only through communicating. It promotes affection and comprehension and aids in relation development. It broadens the understanding of the cosmos and enhances the value of life.

Significance of communication in business

Every conversation that people convey or get for administrative purposes such as operating a business, management of the company, official activities of a non-profit organization, etc.

are referred to as "business communication." Compared to interpersonal and societal correspondence, business communication is characterized by formalism.

All firms' ability to communicate effectively and efficiently is a major factor that determines their achievement. It occurs between business enterprises, markets, and market locations, inside of organizations, different groups of the workforce, leaders and staff, purchasers and sellers, key suppliers and clients, sales representatives and prospects, as well as between individuals within the organization and the press. These communications affect business. When handled carefully, these interactions could advance commercial objectives. If not, it would reflect poorly on the company and could harm business interests.

The communicating system in every foundation has always been its lifeline, which primarily serves to bring about transformation and conduct. Managing an efficient method of communication is a fundamental challenge in every firm. Deprived communication is typically the outcome of operational issues. Commands are misinterpreted, which leads to major errors. The fundamental issue with communicating is that what has been genuinely comprehended might differ from what the other person meant to say. The communication which is passed between the speaker and the listening person could well be distorted by a variety of factors because they are two independent people with distinct limits.

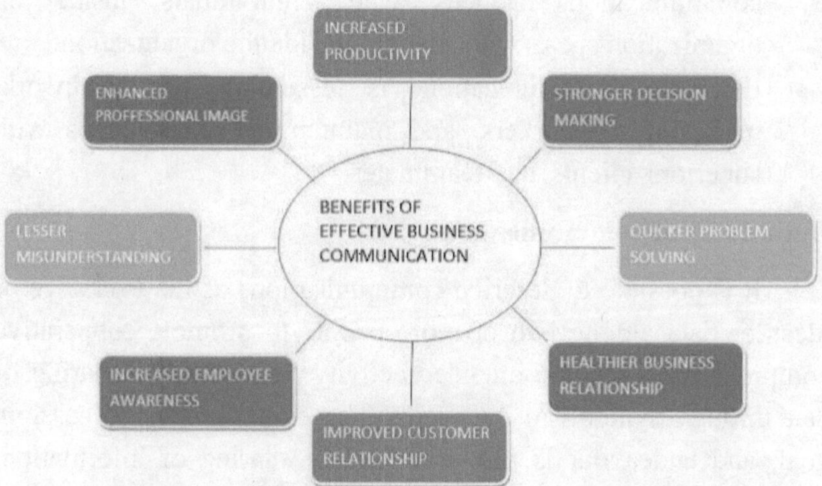

Figure 1: Significance of business communication

Interior communication happens when individuals inside an enterprise interact with one another. They do this to collaborate and achieve their shared objectives. It might be authorized or prohibited. Frontal and writing modes are both forms of communication occurring internally. Instances of interior communication include memoranda, documents, office orders, circulars, faxes, video conferences, meetings, etc.

Exterior communication is the exchange of information between organizational members and anybody from outside. Such persons could be users or consumers, traders or suppliers, the press, the government, or the broader community.

- Communication is essential to the operation of every company. Without an efficient communication infrastructure, none of the firms might grow.

- Regardless of the type of business or magnitude, communications seem to be the foundation that binds an organization intact.

- Communication occurs internally when individuals inside an organization speak with one another, whereas exterior communication happens when individuals inside an organization speak with anyone outside the organization.

- Effective communication is essential for teamwork, managing co-workers, and maintaining relationships with superiors, clients, and teammates.

Definitions of communication

It is possible to describe communications as the exchange of ideas or data among two or more people to promote cooperative comprehension and the intended activity. It entails the sharing of data through symbolism or words. The commonality of passion, goal, and endeavour is produced by the sharing of information, opinions, and perspectives.

"Communication" is defined by the American Managerial Association as "all activities that result in an interchange of meanings."

According to Peter Little, communication is the procedure whereby data is exchanged among people and/or organizations to produce a comprehensible reply. Communication is defined by Newman and Summer Jr. as "an interchange of evidence, thoughts, views or attitudes by two or more people.

As per Keith Davis, 'The method of imparting knowledge and comprehension through one individual to another. In essence, it serves as a bridge of meanings for the population. One could securely traverse the stream of miscommunication by utilizing the bridging'.

According to Louis A. Allen, communicating is the summation of every action an individual performs to foster comprehension in the minds of others. It entails a methodical, ongoing trend of communicating by speaking, hearing, and comprehending.

As a result, the major goal of communication is to enlighten, and persuade others to adopt a particular viewpoint, or motivate them to take action.

Features of communication

- ❖ Fundamentally, communicating is a two-sided procedure. The input we receive determines whether the communication is successful or unsuccessful. Feedback is therefore pivotal to interaction.

- ❖ Throughout all managerial levels along with all types of companies, communicating is a continual activity that is vital. None of the supervisors could do his or her duties effectively if they are unable to interact. Companies that value professionalism and results are constantly searching for executives with strong communication skills.

- ❖ In communications, thoughts and sentiments are just as important as facts. Sayings alone are only a tiny part of communication. More message is frequently conveyed via tone and facial gestures than through speech. With signals, symbolism, and movements, one could convey a lot. A 2-fingered triumph sign, for instance, communicates more effectively than speech.

- ❖ The method of communicating is versatile. It takes into account how the shapes of performers as well as the atmosphere are altering.

- ❖ It is a procedure with objectives. When the recipient and dispatcher are indeed conscious of the communication's aim and that purpose is coherent, collaborating could be productive.

- ❖ Communication is a multidisciplinary field of study wherein, experience gained across multiple disciplines is being utilized. Understanding how people communicate effectively has been assisted by anthropological research (the science of body language), psychological (the science of persuading, cognition, and beliefs), sociological, and political discipline (the science of voting trends).

Goals of communication

The following is a list of primary intentions or purposes of communication:

Guidance: The authoritative aspect is a constant theme in the instructive role. It has a rather directive character. As a result, the interpreter provides a subsequent step with essential instructions and directions to allow a person to carry out his specific job. Here, guidelines generally go from the upper phase to the lesser phase.

Incorporation: It is a condensed activity whereby efforts are made to integrate operations. The primary goal of communication is to establish relationships between several business organizational functionalities. It aids in the fusion of several managerial tasks.

To provide information: In an enterprise, communication serves the objective of informing a person or a group regarding a specific assignment, business policies, processes, etc. Through the medium level, the top managing system communicates policy to the lesser level. The medium level then communicates the lesser level's response to the top level. Throughout the organization, information may move in vertical, horizontal, and diagonal ways. The basic goal of communicating is to update oneself or someone else.

Appraisal: Communication is the process by which actions are examined to generate ideas or render judgments about the value of an activity. A strategy for evaluating the contribution of a person or team to the organization is communication. A suitable and efficient communicating method is required whether assessing one's input, outcomes of others, or even a few ideologies framework.

Direction: Upper executives or a supervisor must communicate with lower levels to give them instructions. Once workers receive guidance from a superior, they will function best. Written or verbal communication can be used to lead each other. Conventional orders, requests orders, and inferred orders are all forms of orders.

Educating: It has been widely accepted how important workplace safeguarding is. To train and instruct employees concerning individual security at work, a thorough communicating approach is necessary. The workforce could save costs, processes, risks, and other issues by communicating effectively.

Impacting: A thorough communicating strategy is required while attempting to persuade someone or when being impacted. A person with the power to affect somebody could readily convince everyone else. It alludes to the giving of a response that reveals the results of the interaction.

To create an image: A company could not exist in isolation from the remainder of the societal structure. Civilization and a business working in society are interconnected as well as dependent on one another. Community assurance and trust must inevitably be built. It may be accomplished through interactions with several sources that must represent the company's image in society. An organization's role is to tell the public about its objectives, initiatives, advancements, and societal responsibilities across an efficient exterior communication network.

Relating to staff configuration: At a certain period, if a new staff member joins the company, she or he won't be familiar with its norms, procedures, cultures, etc. Employees can become more familiar with their superiors, co-workers, and the company's practices, goals, laws, and regulations by communicating with them.

Others: Whenever the decision-maker is given the necessary and sufficient knowledge, an efficient decision-creating is feasible. Creating decisions is made easier when there is good communication. To do duties successfully and efficiently, each person in the business must usually give pertinent details.

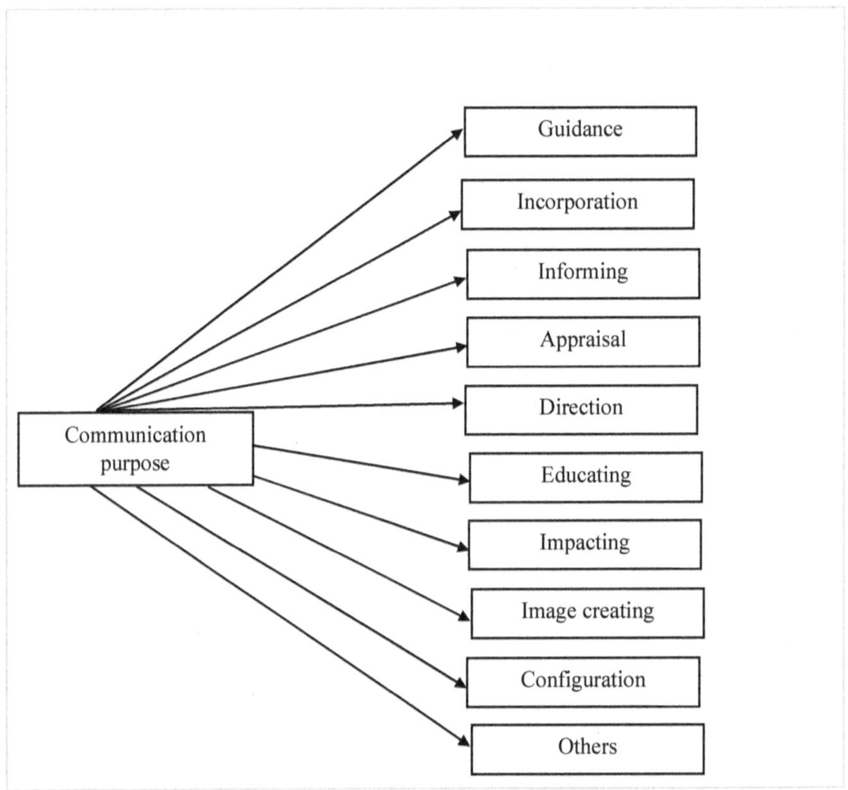

Figure 2: Intention of communication

Situations of communication

Whenever there is a communication situation,

- Someone (the sender or transmitter) wishes to transfer certain info
- The information must be communicated to another individual (the recipient)

- The message conveyed to the recipient is partially or fully understood by him
- The communication is returned or received feedback from the recipient

These four elements are necessary for effective communication.

Importance of Communication

Achievement in business has often depended on communicating effectively. Because of the following factors, communication has subsequently become even more vital:

Size expansion: The size of business organizations has significantly increased. These days, a huge corporation offers numerous employees that operate all over the globe. For the successful completion of its tasks, an effective communication system is necessary.

Rising Specialization: Rigid job segmentation causes various tasks to be performed by multiple agencies. Neither organization could run efficiently with a lack of effective interaction between the various sections to ensure mutual understanding and collaboration. For instance, if the manufacturing and marketing divisions are unable to communicate, the sales force may place an order that the manufacturing dept is unable to accomplish.

Increasingly fierce competitiveness: As a consequence of liberalization and globalization, there is competitive pressure between domestic and international banks. To thrive in the battle of competitiveness, persuasion communication through commercials and personal as well as public interactions will turn out to be important.

Trade unity movement: Employee unions seem to be extremely powerful and influential in enterprises. Along with several issues, the managing system should engage union representatives. Managerial and union representatives can preserve positive relationships by regularly exchanging information and ideas.

Interpersonal relationships: Establishing faith and confidence mutually amongst the workforce and managers necessitates good communication. The involvement of staff in decision-creating and other operations fosters a feeling of commitment and connection across them to the company.

Public affairs: The community demands executives behave responsibly. Businesses must educate the govt, customers, providers, shareholders, and other societal groups concerning their social contributions. Large corporations use specialized professionals for public affairs to assist in business boost and societal reputation.

Personal strength: Effective communication is crucial for achievement across each profession. Executives must give talks, produce documentation and arrange interview sessions. Reception staff, instructors, lawyers, and defenders all require a lot of communication skills.

The process or cycle of communication

The communication process is made up of the sender's thoughts being transmitted to the recipient and the recipient's response to the sender. Whenever an individual (sender) wishes to convey facts, concepts, viewpoints, or other info to another (the recipient), communication is said to have commenced. The sender does have a purpose for such information, concepts, or viewpoints. The message must then be converted or translated into a language that accurately expresses the concept. So, the message needs to be encrypted. The substance of the message, the level of acquaintance of both sender and recipient, as well as other circumstances significantly affect the encoding process.

The message is delivered through the proper network or media after having been encrypted. Conferences, reporting, memoranda, notes, e-mails, faxes, and telephone conversations are frequent communication channels in organizations. When a message is obtained, it is decrypted by the recipient who then informs the sender of whether or not the message in concern has indeed been properly understood.

Communication components

The following components are part of the communication procedure:

Sender or broadcaster: Sender, also referred to as a broadcaster, is the individual who wants to communicate the message. The messaging is started by a sender who also modifies the recipient's conduct.

Message: It is a topic that is covered in all communications. Every fact thought, viewpoint, or informational element might be included. If communication is to occur, it should present within the thoughts of the sender.

Encrypting: The info presenter arranges his thought into a collection of symbols (phrases, signs, and so on.) that he believes it would transmit to the targeted recipient.

Stream of communicating: Sender must choose the route via which to transmit the data. The medium used for communicating is the medium by which the message travels. It serves as the channel between the sender and the recipient.

Recipient: The recipient of a communication is referred to as the receiver or perhaps the individual to whom the transmitter sends a certain statement. In deprived of the presence of the intended recipient, it is impossible to communicate. An individual who gets and attempts to comprehend the communication is the recipient.

Decryption: It is the method of translating information that has been encrypted into its clear meaning. The recipient can extract meaning from a statement with the aid of decryption.

Feedback: Communication is a method of exchanging. For interchange of being accomplished, the sender (or the person who sent basic data) should obtain the return information such that he may learn how the recipient responded. Feedback is the term for the recipient's reaction or response.

Brain drains: It is the term used to describe the probability of misconceptions at any stage during the entire process. This might occur on the behalf of the sender if they select the default stream to convey the message rather than selecting an appropriate media. It could also occur if a recipient improperly decodes the message. In other terms, one might claim that any phase of the cycle has been broken.

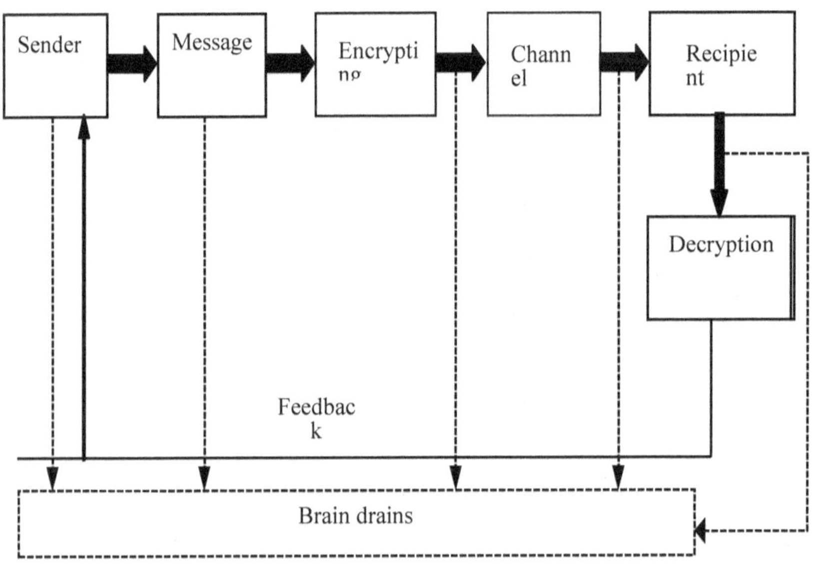

Figure 3: Process of communication

Activity-questions 1

1. How would you describe communication?

2. How do communications play a part in business management?

3. What various goals do communications serve? five of them should be briefly explained.

4. Explain many situations in which communication is possible.

5. "Communicating is the sharing of information, thoughts, feelings, and views between two or more individuals". Discuss the meaning of the statement and the function of feedback in communication.

6. "Communication is a two-sided process." Justify.

7. Explain the various communicating components.

8. List 3 instances of brain drain that occurs in the communicating process.

Chapter-2

Communication and Organization Structure

Communication methods

There are two types of communication: interior and exterior. Exterior communication includes those that take place outdoors of enterprises such as interaction with govt, the community at large or other businesses. Interior communications comprise those that take place within the company and are of two types namely: formal or official and informal.

- **Formal:** All representatives who wish to communicate among themselves must do so through the formal channels that have been established.
- **Informal:** In addition to the formal ways of communicating, each entity does have an informal avenue of communication which is equally compelling. This unofficial network is frequently referred to as a rumour mill since it extends across all three axes—horizontal, vertical, and diagonal—of information exchange. It can be seen when events are held in groupings especially near the water fountain, in dining halls, or down corridors.

Formal communication

Advantages

- It crosses lines of authority and guarantees that responsible leaders remain in positions of obligation and power.
- It facilitates the growth of close relationships between a primary supervisor and his minions.
- It maintains consistency in the way information is shared.
- It has a clear circulation in which the data is reliable.
- Knowing the information's provenance fosters unity among the staff.

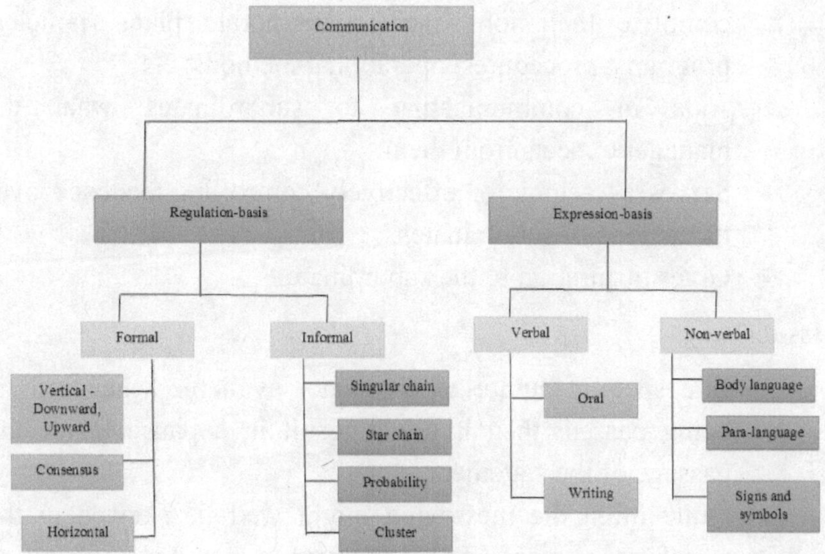

Figure 4: Communication types

Drawbacks

- ➢ Adds the work-loading of different managerial members because communication must pass through them.
- ➢ Broadens the communication barrier across upper-level administrators and low-level workers.
- ➢ This process consumes time since it adheres to the scalar network of authorities. The process of communicating from one level of power to the next is excessively slow.

Downward communication

Downward communication occurs when information passes from an upper to a lower level. It includes orders, specific directives, policy suggestions, circulars, and other things.

Advantages

> Assists in providing minions with the info they need to complete their jobs such as corporate plans, policies, programs, procedures, operational methods, etc.

> Aids in communicating to subordinates what the manager expects from them.

> Serves as a tool for effectively controlling feedback over the actions of subordinates.

> Gives inspiration to the subordinate.

Issues

> If a specific authorization is not available when info is being passed, then it might result in a pause inside the passage of the statement.

> Quite often the messaging might well be skewed in the transfer across one level to the next.

> Often an unequal task-load distribution amongst workers results in an overburden or underload of work that makes the workforce unhappy.

Techniques/channels for upper communication

1. With the support of supervisors, subordinates address respective problems via conversation and develop a solution.

2. Workers should write to the managing system regarding any concerns or suggestions they may have regarding the workplace, policies and procedures, peer groups, etc. without providing any personal information by dropping it into the box. The executives routinely examine such gripped boxes to identify problems and their solutions.

3. It works incredibly well for upward communication. The medium of social event in which both supervisors and subordinates gather on a similar site as well as express their

sentiments and thoughts quite conveniently when an organization applauds their annual celebration hosts sporting events for their staff or engages in a certain type of social welfare activity such as planting trees or donating food to storm zones, among other things.

4. It is directly in opposition to the gripped box system. The staff's identity is displayed herein. Every worker has the option of writing directly to a superior stage over an issue they experienced.

5. It places a strong emphasis on human psychology. A superior act as a counsellor and offers advice to workers who are having problems. Counseling not just addresses the issues that workers are currently undergoing; this even discourses prospects and ways to help people for performing more efficiently at their respective jobs.

Strategies for becoming efficient

1. The supervisors must make an effort to build relationships with the employees beneath them.

2. Attempting to communicate informally wherever feasible.

3. Personnel complaints are to be promptly addressed.

The lateral or horizontal communication process

This takes place among individuals within the same organizational structure, whether they are from a similar or distinct dept. or section.

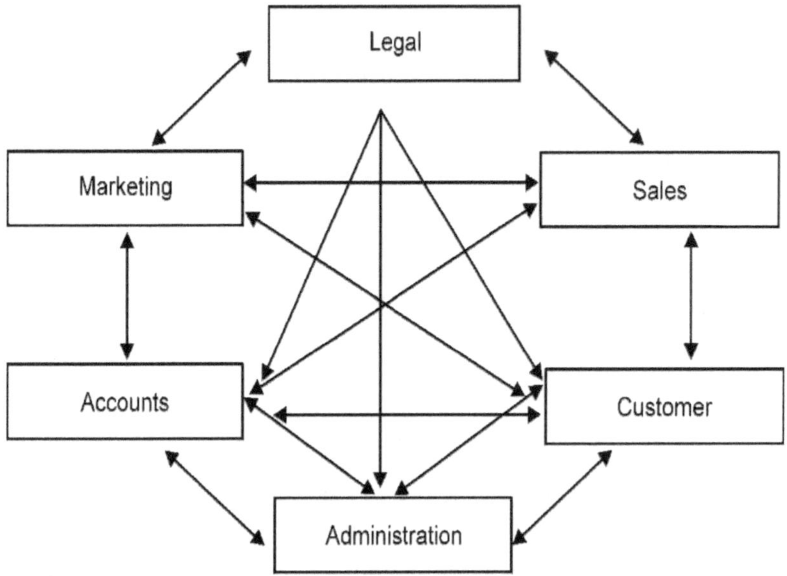

Figure 5: Lateral or horizontal communication

Advantages

- ➢ It establishes mutual faith and trusts across personnel at a common level, which aids in preserving or fostering understanding between those in corresponding positions across distinct divisions.
- ➢ The sense of cooperation across diverse depts would be created or developed if individuals of identical positions interact with one another to achieve a certain goal.

Issues

- ➢ Occasionally, it generates enmity amongst staff members from different depts.
- ➢ Proximity demonstrates the like and dislikes of a worker who is close to each other based on location. Similar to every firm, the market sector and human resources depts are located closer together than the manufacturing ones. Therefore, as opposed to a production plant, HR and the

market sector benefit from their close nearness to one another.

> Bias refers to the tendency to favour or dislike a worker based on factors like their persona, race, ethnicity, or family status.

Horizontal communicating strategies

Face-to-face (F2F) interaction: Straight communication between two people such as F2F contact reduces the likelihood of miscommunication because prompt response improves communication more efficiently.

Telephonic interaction: If personnel is preoccupied with their job or located wide apart from one another, a telephone conversation is more appropriate than a F2F interaction. Although it takes less time, occasionally disturbances as well as other impediments cause delays and skew the information.

Regular meetings: Regular meetings would be those which are held on a weekly, monthly, quarterly, or yearly basis with personnel to address predefined topics.

Memo: Memos are a writing way of communicating that is passed across various depts within a company. This also refers to an intra-official letter.

Consensus

A consensus is achieved if a group of individuals, regardless of their status gather and consult each other to choose a solution that will be accepted by everyone. Such communication will follow a fixed format that can't be changed.

Consensus with the consulting process

1. Main executive carries on the issue and investigates it.

2. Gather further data and facts.

3. Look for different ways to resolve it.

4. Look for substitutes.

5. Executive makes personal calls to each member or extends an invitation to a gathering.

6. Members are informed of the issue.

7. To thoroughly hear each member's perspective.

8. Concluded.

Advantages

> Members discover it simple to embrace decisions that have been reached following discussions with numerous parties.
> It fosters unity among team participants. If there is any disagreement or divide among the members, it shall be thoroughly identified and attempted to be resolved

Drawbacks

> Member is pushed into endorsing a position he disagrees with.
> On occasion, it could give the wrong impression of administration to members who believe that managing might not be capable of solving effectively their issue.

Informal or grapevine communication

Contributing aspects for grapevine phenomena

1. A sense of assurance or an absence of guidance while a company is going through a troubling time.

2. A sense of inadequacies or loss of faith among workers, which results in the construction of gaps.

3. The establishment of a club or preferred grouping by executives, which causes other staff to feel uneasy or alone.

Grapevine communicating kinds

Solitary chain: Under this form of a chain, "A" talks about some topic with "B," who then "says" "C" and so on. Communication of this kind may travel sequentially or in a single strand from one individual to other. When "A" talks "B" about anything, then "B" afterward informs "C" and the cycle continues. A noteworthy finding from such a method of communicating is that whenever each individual conveys specific info to the next, they perceive information as private or hidden, wherein also another individual then communicates with a similar sense of privacy.

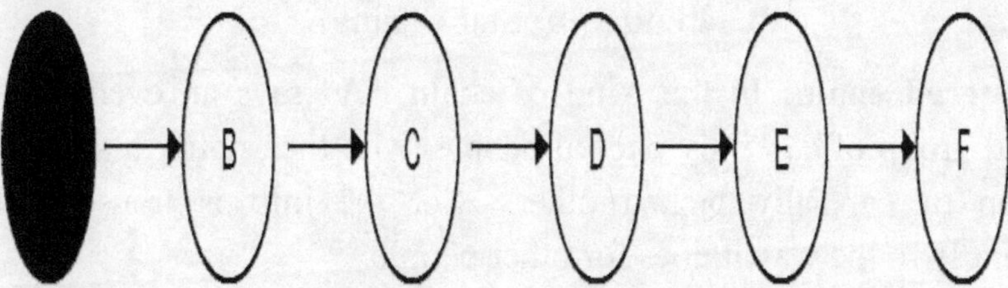

Figure 6a: Solitary Chain

Star chain: In this kind of circuit, each member tells up and shares the info they have learned with the group. For conveying a message or a statement about an intriguing yet unrelated work sort, this chain is frequently employed. It is occasionally referred to as a gossiping chain.

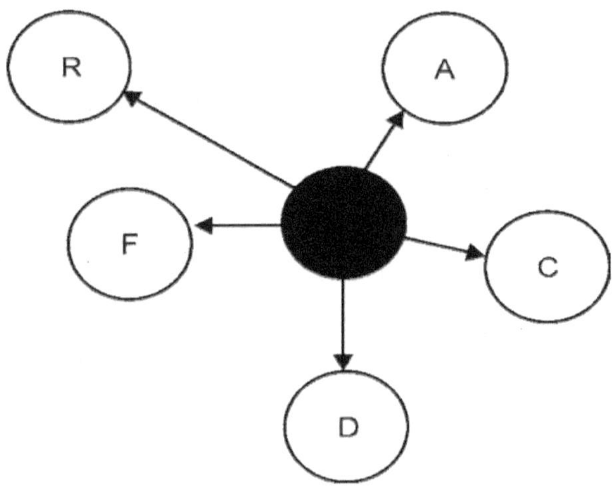

Figure 6b: Star Chain

Clustered chain: In this kind of chain, "A" says an event to a small group of carefully chosen people, who then notify a smaller group of carefully picked others. So, the info is transmitted similarly to the way it does for other people.

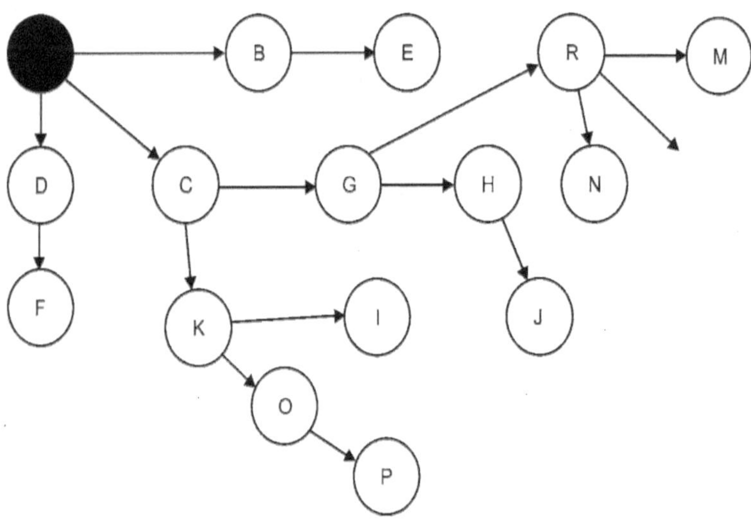

Figure 6c: Clustered chain

Probabilistic chain: This chain is a possible system wherein knowledge is sent to another as per the rules of probabilities and these individuals subsequently notify even more people in the same way. This type can also be referred to as a randomized chain.

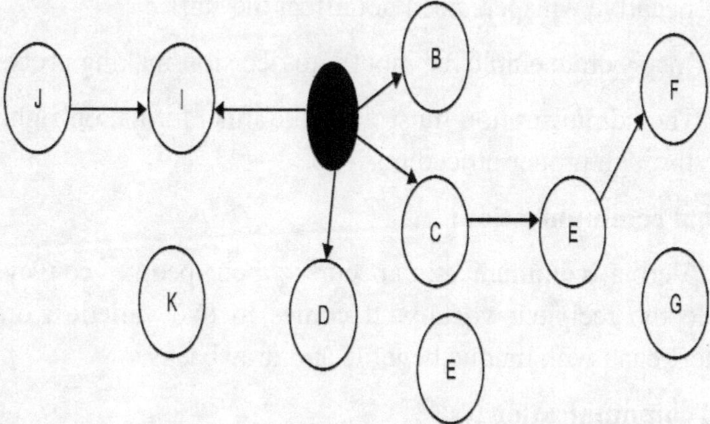

Figure 6d: Probabilistic chain

Advantages

> Due to the way that groups are formed—based on personal preferences of likes or dislikes, the grapevine allows for the fastest possible message transmission.
> It supports additional communication channels.
> This kind of communication produces feedback promptly.
> Whenever people talk among themselves through the grapevine, the group's members become more coherent and retain unity.
> Workers experience psychological comfort from employing grapevine interaction. Since they can speak with one another with no fear of greater authorities or a sense of inferiority.

Drawbacks

> There seems to be a high likelihood that team members will misinterpret messages.
> Information transfer is dependent on the readiness of senders as well as their employed grapevine approach, which occasionally results in the delivery of partial data.

Strategies for becoming efficient

1. Managerial need to look out for the leaders. Consequently, the negative whispers need not affect the staff.

2. Incorporate employee input into decision-making processes.

3. The administration must deny the misinformation right away through proper procedures.

Verbal communication:

Verbal communication occurs when people convey their info to the recipient vocally. It comes in two varieties: oral and written, each with unique benefits and drawbacks.

Oral communication

Oral communication occurs when a statement or info is exchanged using uttered phrases. Either F2F communication or mechanical technologies may be employed.

Written communication

Communication that takes place by writing means such as a letter, telegraphing, faxing, or emails is known as written communication. It ensures that all parties involved are informed consistently. It gives a permanent recording of all communications for the future. If the action required is critical and difficult, writing directions are important. Interaction through writing must be clear, concise, accurate, and complete to be effective.

Non-verbal communication:

The technique of communicating via the transmission and reception of voiceless signals is commonly characterized as non-verbal interaction. This information could be conveyed by motion, pose, body language, facial expression, eye contact, or even via the use of objects such as dresses, haircuts, architecture, icons, and info graphical ways. Paralinguistic components like vocal qualities, attitude, and speech patterns along with phonation characteristics like rhythm, tone, and tension might also be present in speaking. Similar to spoken language, writings also contain non-vocal components including handwritten form, phrase placement, and emotional expression.

Blockades of the communication process:

Incorrect media selection

Every message needs to be delivered from the proper media. Among the major obstacles to communicating is poor media. Instances like situations where depts or divisions are spread out within a large entity make interaction difficult. When a supervisor needs to speak privately with someone, writing correspondence is the preferred method over other forms of communication. Therefore, the media must be precise. If improper or inappropriate media is chosen, it creates a major obstacle to communicating.

Physical blockades

- **Noise**— In factories, the annoying machinery noise makes oral communication problematic.
  Electrical noise obstructs telephonic and speaker communications.
  Every tangible interruption including poor handwriting, substandard printouts, etc., is also considered noise.
- **Distance and timing:**

  — Overcrowding in telecom and networking infrastructure.

  — Employees who work various shifts.

  — A room's incorrect seating preparation.

Table 1: Blockades of communication

Communicating blockades			
Incorrect media selection	**Physical**	**Semantic**	**Social and psychological**
- Ideal choice of medium based on circumstances plays a vital role	- Noise - Distance and timing	- Interpreting - Bypassed - Connotative and Denotative	- Beliefs and attitudes - Feelings - Locked mind - Position-awareness - Information source - Flaw transmission - Deprived retention

Semantic blockades

- **Word interpreting**

An individual may understand the same term differently which could put a hurdle inside the process of communicating. In the publication "Effective Business Communication," Murphy and Peck noted that the diminutive term "run" possess

71 meanings as a verb

35 as noun

4 more as an adjective.

- **Bypassing directives**

When the transmitter of messages as well as the recipient ascribe distinct interpretations to the identical term or utilize varied phrases to convey similar meaning is referred to as a bypass.

"Bring it to the storage room and burn it"

In official terminology, burning refers to 'making additional copies of similar documentation'.

- **Connotation and Denotation**

Words can have either a connotation or denotation meaning.

Denotation - A phrase's denotation meaning is its actual definition. It should provide information and identify items by not making favourable or unfavourable judgments.

Connotation: It permits qualitative assessments as well as individual responses.

Like — true, affordable, genuine, etc.

Example — "He provided us with inexpensive stuff."
"Items are cheaply priced here."
The 1st one has a positive connotative, and the latter has a negative one.
The following could be utilized to circumvent such issue (via way of transmitted instructions as well as connotative definitions of words):

- ❖ Choose the language that the recipient will appreciate.
- ❖ When using terms that are unaware to the recipient, it is indeed essential to render their clearer meanings instantly.
- ❖ One ought to use terms with good connotations instead of negative ones.

Social and psychological blockades

- **Beliefs and attitudes**

    The information which supports a person's thoughts and attributes is preferable to that specific person.

- **Feelings**

    It plays an important role in the act of communication. The sender won't be capable of structuring his message effectively if he is confused, anxious, frightened, enthusiastic, scared, or tense.

- **Locked mind**

    Communication with someone who has a blocked mentality can be quite challenging. They simply won't respond because of adamant about their viewpoint.

- **Position-awareness**

    People avoid being honest because they are very mindful of their superior or inferior status.

- **Information source**

    Our responses are based on how much faith we have in the communicating origin.

- **Flaw transmission**

    The information is largely lost during transportation. Approximately somewhat in the sequence of 30percentage of transmitted data orally is missed during every transmission.

- **Deprived retention**

    Given the limited individual recall capacity, oral messages in particular tend to be missed.(Around 50percentage of info is retained by workers)

Standards of significant communication

Making a detailed listing of the essential components of the communication process is highly challenging. This would rely upon particular requirements of circumstance. To develop excellent interaction, one can adhere to the rules or standards below:

Figure 7: Standards of effective communication

Clarity of message

It is the cornerstone of effective interaction. There should be no ambiguity in the statement. There ought to be no uncertainty inside it. Only if it is explicitly indicated within the minds of both sender and recipient, then it is possible to be transmitted effectively.

Speediness

An efficient communicating approach needs to provide quick data transfer. Depending on how urgently the information needs to be communicated, the length of time it takes for a statement to travel to its destiny as well as the speediness of communicating network must be taken into consideration.

Dual-way procedure

Communicating is a dual-way procedure that allows the recipient to give feedback to the sender. Responses seem to be the dissemination of knowledge regarding the outcome of every communicating act.

Reliability

Belief serves as the foundation for communication. The output as a part of expertise will create this environment. The transmitter should be trusted by the recipient. He should have great respect for the outlet's expertise in the area.

Comprehensiveness

All communications should be both sufficient and thorough. Inadequate communications cause misunderstandings, leave the recipient in dark, and postpone the taking of action.

Contents

The content should be relevant to the recipient and consistent with his core values. It should mean something to him. People typically choose the info or services that will offer the biggest incentives to them. The reaction of viewers is influenced by the content.

Accurateness

The communicating channel must assure message delivery accuracy. Any media selected by the sender must be correct for the specific type of data they intend to deliver.

Capacity

When communicating, one should consider the capabilities of the viewer. Whenever receivers have to exert the smallest amount of effort, communications are indeed successful. This involves elements such as reading comprehension and audience familiarity.

Economic system: The communicating network ought to be as cost-effective as is practical. However, to attain an economy, the effectiveness of service must not be compromised.

Confidentiality

The communication system must provide privacy as well as prevent data leakage. If information is secret, it becomes significantly more important

Bridges for efficient communication:

Developing and maintaining a system of communication is the key job of any manager. The characteristics of a good communication system are discussed below:

1. **Dual-way channel:** When communicating, there seem to be 2 groups associated: the initiator or sender statements and the recipient. Two modes of communication are necessary for better communication. It ought to be horizontal, down, and upwards. As a result, a supervisor must be able to hear, comprehend as well as do interpretation in addition to providing information, instructions, and orders.

2. **Transparency of message:** Before talking, the communicators ought to have clarification of facts, thoughts, and opinions in mind. In the opinion of Koontz and Donnell, "A communication has clearness if it is represented in a linguistic and delivered in such a fashion which could be understood by the recipient."

3. **Mutual trustworthiness:** Whenever the sender and the recipient of information have respect or comprehension mutually, a communicating system might well be deemed efficient. A strong communication network in every dept or

entity is indicated by the presence of positive intrapersonal relationships among superiors as well as their minions.

4. **On-time messaging:** Communication's timely delivery must receive careful consideration. Nothing is more harmful than outdated information.

5. **Messaging uniformity:** The communicator could accomplish consistent quality by remembering the company's goals, standards, and programs. It must not disagree with earlier statements because doing so can cause chaos and uncertainty within the business.

6. **Good relationships:** The communicating method must be selected so that it will not offend the recipient. This must foster accurate comprehension of the recipient in their thoughts, resulting in the development and maintenance of a positive connection between the sender and recipient.

7. **Feedback:** It helps the recipient to interpret the message correctly. It is useful in establishing 2-way communication. The sender should make an effort to establish if the recipient fully comprehended the information.

8. **Adaptability:** The communication method needs to be adaptable enough to change with the demands. Novel forms of communicating ought to be easily absorbed by it.

Seven Cs of communication

The overall 7 Cs of communication are illustrated below figure.

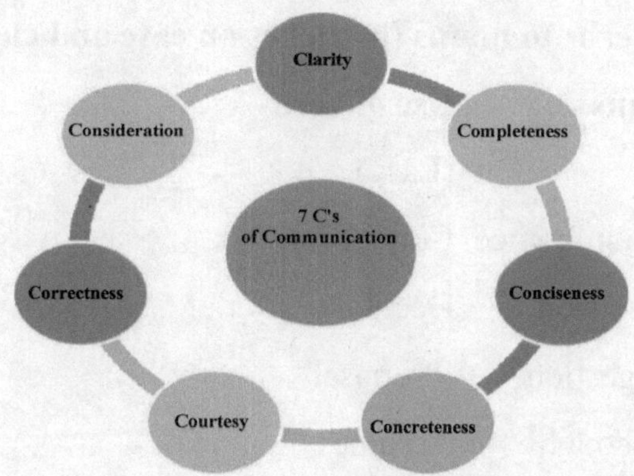

Figure 8: Seven Cs of communication

Seven Cs of writing communication:

1. Clarity

Clear thinking: It results from a thorough assessment of the communication's goal, message, and media.

Expression clearness:

1. Use simplified, understandable language:

Avoiding	Use
Compensation	Payment
Enabling	Helping
Utilized	Used

2. For lengthy sentences, use solitude words:

Lengthy phrase	Solitude term
Every time	Continuous
For the need of	For
Before	Earlier
On account	Since

3. Apply verbs to nouns (it fetches on ease and clearness):

Use of nouns	Use of verbs
(Tough)	(Easy)
Came to an inference	Conclusion
Create a decision	Decide
Give a suggestion	Proposal
Take into thought	Assume

4. Remove dual entries

Dual entries	Simplified
Real facts	Facts
Ending effect	Results
Time of 1 week	1 week
Prior knowledge	Knowledge

5. Avoid uncertainty: if the information has higher than one possible interpretation. There is uncertainty because of false punctuation.

Go. slow working under progress

Go slow. working under progress

6. Use brief language: Limit the ideas to one line. It is advisable to divide a phrase into 2 if it is longer than 30 characters.

2. Completeness

When responding to a letter or communicating with someone else, ensure that the user has addressed all of their questions.

Inspection for five w's queries.

- What
- Who
- Where

- When

- Why

3. Conciseness

- Inclusion of solely appropriate truths

- Avoiding recurrence

- Well-organized messaging.

4. Consideration

- Adopting of you-attitude

We-attitude	You-attitude
I have to convey my	Thanking for
Sincere gratitude for	your kind words.
Positive remarks	

- Avoiding gender biases

Avoid	Use
Chairman	Chairperson
Policeman	Police Sir/Madam

5. Courtesy

One should cultivate familiarity with everyone to whom they write to conduct business. Friendly nature and courtesy go with each other.

- Respond to letters right away.

- Leave out annoying phrases.

(You were negligent, careless, and ignorant).

- Express honest regret for a mistake or heartfelt gratitude for a benefit.

6. Correctness

• Present accurate data.

• Use the right timing when sending a text.

• Use appropriate style when messaging.

7. Concreteness

• Use precise facts and statistics at all times.

• Messaging must be clear and appealing.

• Resist exaggerating.

Figure 9: 7 Cs of writing communication

7 Cs of oral communication:

Francis J. Bergin asserts that an oral communicator needs to keep in mind the 7 Cs.

These include the following:

1. **Clearness:** Oral communication is productive whenever the intended message of the transmitter is understood by the audience or recipient. As a result of the presenter's difficulty in speaking clearly, oral communications are frequently misinterpreted. Therefore, good pronouncing skill is vital for

such a goal. A person speaking attempts to practice various, longer, and unique terms for clear pronunciation to reduce these types of issues.

2. **Concise:** Numerous persons relish conversing; thus, oral communication can occasionally struggle with the issue of higher communication. However, if the person who is speaking talks for a lengthy time, his or her point would be lost.

3. **Completion:** Similar to writing communication, completion is necessary for communicating orally as well. As one speaks with others, one is to be careful for keeping in mind the following queries. It must be sure to examine the 5 W's queries:

- Who

- What

- When

- Were

- Why

4. **Correction:** Correction in oral communication refers to the accuracy of information's origin as well as its reliability. Since if the informational resource is reliable, other people will trust towards speaking persons and pay close attention to what they have to say.

5. **Concrete:** The speaker must resist embellishing certain data and instead employ particular facts as well as concepts to make orally an efficient communicating path. They make an effort to select suitable terms that do not negatively impact a specific person, civilization, religion, or country.

6. **Courtesies:** Showing respect requires one's attitude. Utilize courteous language while speaking. Strives to avoid using annoying phrases, needs to apologize for any errors, and

avoids using any racial, ethical, national, or other forms of discrimination-related utterances.

7. **Candidness:** Whenever a communicator opts for a candid strategy, their messaging must be direct, honest, and forthright. Yet without harming a specific person.

Activity-questions 2

1. What forms of communication are there? Compose thorough notes on the significance, benefits, and drawbacks of any 2 of them.

2. Specify formal communication. Explain both its advantages and disadvantages.

3. What are the various kinds of formal communication? Describe any 2 of them in brief.

4. What are the advantages and disadvantages of consensus?

5. Compose a brief essay on unofficial (informal) communication.

6. How many varieties of grapevine are there? Describe with instances.

7. Make a note of communicating:

    (i) Upward

    (ii) Downward

    (iii) Horizontal

    (iv) Grapevine

    (v) Consensus

8. Explain the benefits of unofficial communication in business settings.

9. Describe the formal channels of communicating in a business entity as explanatory notes.

10. Differentiate between upward and downward communication by using instances.

11. What kind of blockades will hinder information exchange inside a company?

12. Explain semantic blockades to proper communication and how they can be removed.

13. What are the various kinds of social and psychological blockades exist towards communicating?

14. Describe how choosing the incorrect media might block the successful communication process.

15. Which sort of physical aspects can make communicating difficult?

16. Make short notes about:

(i) Conscious status

(ii) Beliefs and attitudes

(iii) Feelings

(iv) Locked mind

(v) Deprived retention

(vi) Flaw transmission

(vii) Information source

17. Describe the basic concepts of proper communication.

18. Explain the gateway for communicating effectively.

19. Describe the 7 Cs of writing communication.

20. Describe the 7 Cs of communicating orally.

21. Explain the significance of clear messaging in writing communication.

22. Make notes about messaging given:

(i) Clearness

(ii) Completion

(iii) Courtesy

(iv) Correction

✳✳✳

Unit-II

Organizations And Communication In The

Chapter- 1

Culture And Communication Within The Organization

Communications and organization culture expression

Context

The cultures of organizations can be represented in many distinct methods. The mission statements of the company, which may also be defined as a collection of principles, frequently serve as a representation of the formal organizational culture. Hewlett-Packard is the source of what has been referred to as "the most prominent collection of organizational standards in the US.

Top management can merely publicize and disseminate such slogans with ease. If the company does not measure to such statements, as stated, workers will become highly cynical very fast, particularly if they are widely advertised. The administration of Hewlett-Packard sincerely believes in the organization's corporate principles, and it has been suggested that its day-to-day business practices appropriately express and symbolize these beliefs. This is among the basic causes for the firm's continued achievement, it has been said. A company must therefore try its utmost to uphold its cultural norms if it declares them.

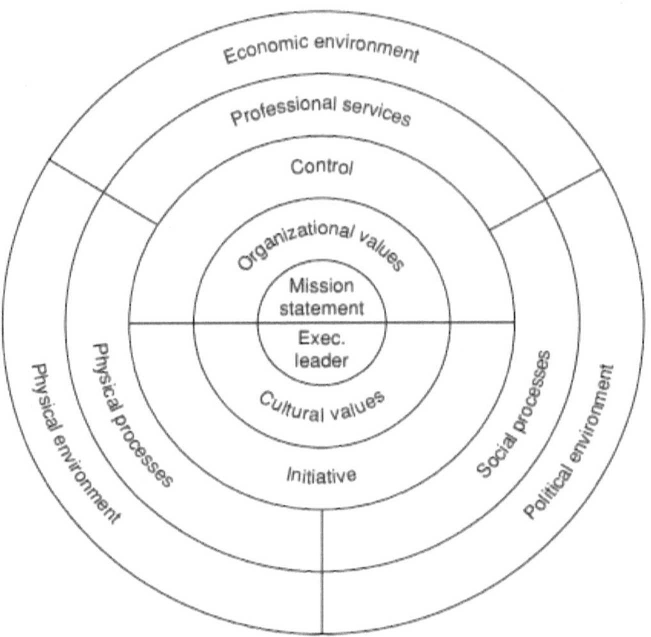

Figure 10: Factors that affect organizational culture

How corporate culture might be exposed in more intimate contact has attracted the interest of investigators more and more. Research has been done, for instance, on how individuals utilize catchphrases and slogans within organizations, how graffiti is used within organizations, how jokes about organizations spread, how individuals define their experiences within organizations using metaphors, and how individuals tell tales about protagonists within organizations.

Investigation into these topics can show the ideals that the organization's participants uphold as well as any potential disagreement between subgroups. We may use certain real-world examples of ways various methods of reflecting on organizational culture can be used to exemplify this type of study.

A young person from a low-income peasant household who started an automobile maintenance shop in Korea after World War II founded the Hyundai Organization. He was regarded as a terrifying apparition at the peak of his abilities. According to one of the legends surrounding him, a stretcher was utilized to be maintained in the executive chamber and was available for use anytime he would "knock out underlings" who were hesitant to accomplish.

Numerous conventional publications on organizational life are criticized by Yiannis Gabriel and Stephen Fineman for providing a very fixed and sterile portrayal of organizational reality. They invited young individuals to recollect one event or discussion that best exemplified what it seemed to perform for their position, and the result is a collection of 45 anecdotes in their publication. Regarding this, Gabriel and Fineman make a note, pointing out that these accounts are not meant to be numerically significant and that they have been gathered at a period when numerous British companies were undergoing significant transformation and reorganization. The takeaway from this is that businesses would be well to focus extra emphasis on communication during hard or challenging economic times. In challenging circumstances, the organization requires each individual to be working their hardest. These instances indicate methods that poor managerial communication may weaken employee dedication. Another thing to note is that in these tales, we just have "one half of the event."

The metaphor's potency

The analysis of employment-management disputes at Disneyland is a prime illustration of the metaphor's potency in a major business enterprise. Smith and Eisenberg implied that Disneyland constituted a "play" and a "family" from their examination of worker surveys that these two basic metaphors best described the Disney strategy. Users were referred to as the "audience" by workers who considered themselves as "performers" putting on "outfits" to perform a "play" for them. When describing administration or employee interactions and attitudes, the familial metaphor was often employed. The staff perceived a break in Disney's compassion concept when management implemented harsh economic actions in response to growing competition. Smith and Eisenberg subsequently went on to talk about how the administration may "re-evaluate" these metaphors to persuade workers that a new strategy was necessary. This opens the door to the prospect of promoting novel cultural norms to assist organizational change, a subject we will back to in Part 5.

Tales Vs collections

The evaluation of organizations is another recurring issue in the research on organizational culture. According to Browning (1992), the inclination for collections or tales can be used to distinguish between 2 major cultural groups. To instruct its personnel on what to accomplish and how to perform it, the "collections" company will frequently provide documented records. This represents the ideals of the organization, which include the upholding of norms, responsibility, certainty, and so on. The "tales" organization, in contrast, will depend on direct communication with staff members and storytelling. This is a group that appreciates comedy, drama, and performance.

Difference in culture

The majority of organizational storytelling studies today have focused on Western businesses with English as their primary language. The organization's participants might use tales to represent themselves differently in diverse cultures. For instance, research on story-telling in a Malaysian organization discovered that most tales utilized conventional classics and chronological protagonists, whereas tales in British or US organizations frequently utilize pictures, funny stories, and metaphors derived from famous broadcast shows, movies, and songs. A narrative where the Power Rangers protagonists were employed to remark on present administration concerns was the only significant outlier.

Executive views, organization ideals, cultural values, and the mission

The organization's aim or objective needs to be at the hub of its culture, according to the concept. However, if 3 more factors—executive views, organizational ideals, and cultural values—do not "echo" this objective, this might not be the situation. Dispute of a certain kind is unavoidable if the 4 components are not in harmony.

All organizations need to strike an equilibrium between opposing instincts to keep supervision on the one side and to promote innovation on the other. It gets more problematic as the organization gets bigger. This is an extremely critical subject to explain because everyone in the organization needs to "understand where they belong" on these problems.

Conclusion

There are 2 significant connections connecting culture and communication. First, communication is a vehicle through which culture is sometimes subtly communicated. Secondly, the communication's subject matter represents certain organizational cultural norms. Business culture can be conceptualized in a variety of forms and at various stages, and there are various frameworks for it. Business culture can possess extremely obvious and significant operational repercussions, regardless of its exact description. For instance, it may have a significant effect on staff motivation and the way the business reacts to transformation. The "formal" business culture is used to communicate and exhibit organizational culture. The purpose or values declaration of the organization frequently serves as a representation of this. If the organization does not measure to such statements, particularly if they are widely publicized, workers will grow highly sceptical very fast. How organizational culture can be exposed in more intimate communication, like storytelling, has drawn growing interest from investigators. According to this study, these communication channels frequently serve to emphasize the differences between the firm's "public image" and how its personnel views its ideals. Organizational culture is influenced or determined by a variety of circumstances, including the political climate. It's crucial to consider how these things combine.

Chapter-2
Communication and Technology

The technological advancement functions

In this day of communication, having accessibility to a lot of info is regarded as prosperity. The use of information-retrieving methods, which have made significant contributions to the development of modern communication technologies, is among the foundations of this type of resource.

Given extensive corporate business activities, the application of novel communication technologies can address a few of the fundamental issues, including precision, expense, velocity, quality, and volume. Therefore, in today's complicated commercial organizations, where communication must reach a broad geographical area both in and out of the nation, the need for alternate means has become essential. In numerous businesses, communication methods other than the usual ones including television, radio, computers, sound/visual tapes, video discs, telecommunications, and numerous mechanical components have been utilized effectively. They are beneficial for administrative tasks like organization, management, guidance, and incentive, among others.

It would be challenging to remain in the competitive environment if the business does not utilize new technology for purpose of communication to assist the population as a societal obligation.

Figure 11: Communication network

Everything that takes the shape of the Internet and might have numerous lines connecting one another is referred to as a "network." A network in the context of a computer setting refers to a link between several machines both inside and exterior the company. A collection of linked nodes or routes that can communicate with one another makes up an electronic network. Possible business norms are the linkage of numerous electronics or peripheral equipment at dispersed places that send data required to carry out network operations. The network of electronic communication is the linking of all different channels. A well-connected computer network, therefore, considers multiple pathways. It stands for a unified operating system, then. A contemporary complicated organization may include several dispersing sites linked by other sites, which suggests the possibility of a network.

Networking characteristics

1. It aids in establishing and sustaining exterior communication using a third-party organization.

2. Recasts management as a function and completely changes the manager's job.

3. Professionals in any area can communicate with one another.

4. Increasing staff productivity allows for the eventual goal of fostering networking within the company to be accomplished.

5. The availability, real-time nature, and ongoing improvement of the informational caliber of business data.

6. It expands the number of devices or endpoints connected and enables the communication between the set of networks and particular networks.

7. The network system enables data to be distributed in a timely, rapid, and effective manner, especially in the situation of multinational organizations with a worldwide workforce that operates in numerous different nations.

Networking benefits

1. It is quick and simple to exchange data between multiple electronics.

2. Fast and simple accessibility to data and its instant availability aid in boosting output.

3. It reduces the amount of work required to complete documentation.

4. As F2F engagement is made possible by technologies; it spares workers a significant amount of effort and time.

5. It is simple to notify all of the dispersed personnel about any modifications to organizational policies or procedures.

Intranet

The term "intranet" refers to a link to the web within the company. It is also known as a platform having a limited population. Selected personnel inside the organization receive well-managed and organized data via the intranet platform. The internet can be accessed via the intranet, yet not the other way around. Entry to the intranet is constrained or exclusive. Intra alludes to personal networking within a company. Intra implies within and about electronic networks.

An intranet is an inner webpage utilized by a company to provide business-based data and information to workers. Numerous businesses have been looking for new strategies to enhance staff communication in recent times. To distribute content more effectively and thereby cut down on overhead expenses, the deployment, and use of the intranet is indeed a viable alternative.

Intranet Benefits

1. Reduces the expense of business communication by up to 60%.

2. Raises workers' levels of effectiveness and production.

3. It gives individuals a means of quickly getting the knowledge they require whenever they require it.

4. Regardless of the hardware technologies they use, every employee of an organization has the chance to use the intranet's technologies and to view the data held by the business.

5. The intranet transforms the traditional paper workplace into an electronic workplace by producing electronic files for possible business communication.

6. Intranets reduce obstacles to open communication within organizations, enabling both people and groups to interact and exchange information.

INTERNET & INTRANET

Figure 12: Internet & intranet

Internet

The abbreviation "net" is used to refer to the global network now known as the internet. The internet is made up of several tiny networks and other, smaller, globally dispersed linked computers. The world wide web and cyberspace are accessible through it. So, it is an international network of interconnected, autonomous computer groupings. Two-way communication is possible on the internet. A customer's computer screen becomes a window to the entire globe as they explore the internet's possibilities. The transmitter and the recipient must be located on a similar system line for the Net to function.

To describe it plainly, the internet can be compared to the telephone network, which also serves as a means of international communication. Connecting to the Internet can be done in numerous different methods. Likewise, various kinds of programs can be run. A channel or means for numerous systems to connect is the Internet. A product's integrity and ability to compete and offer on the global marketplace determine its performance in the industry. The existence of a given product featuring precise characteristics, cost, usability, and other attributes must be made known to the possible worldwide user in a worldwide marketing arrangement.

Benefits of the internet

1. Messages can be sent and received worldwide over the internet.

2. Having data saved on the systems for later use.

3. Perusing periodicals like magazines and newspapers.

4. Obtaining content that we find interesting, including publications.

5. Using e-banking, which is the practice of managing one's bank account via email.

6. Online shopping allows consumers to conserve time.

7. Upgrades one business with the most recent technologies available worldwide.

E-mail

Using a system of telecommunication and computer connections, customers can receive and send information using electronic mail, or e-mail, a network of electronic communication. The message could be composed of brief remarks and congratulations, lengthy text documents with visuals and photographs, video recordings, or sound, or just plain content. Email is an "electronic post office" because of this. Even without a receiver on the other side, it enables communication. It entails that one can deliver emails whenever the user wishes and at any moment. The recipient of the text may read it anytime he or she chooses. As a result, for that specific communication, the transmitter and the recipient do not need to interact at the identical moment.

E-mail benefits

1. It makes it possible to transmit and receive messages from people who have email addresses.

2. It almost quickly sends the message. It moves quite quickly as a result.

3. It isn't necessary to necessitate the recipient of the communication to be there on the other side. The recipient can examine the information by accessing his mailbox at any moment to see if it has been delivered to him.

4. It is delivered immediately to the recipient's email.

5. It guarantees a better level of information secrecy.

6. It is an incredibly inexpensive form of communication. Email can frequently take the place of written correspondence like letters and memos.

7. Since messages can be transmitted at any moment, daytime or nighttime, time zone issues are less of an issue.

8. Multiple recipients can receive the same message at once.

Etiquettes of e-mail

1. Quick reply to email communications.

2. For the ease of the recipient, give every email a subject line.

3. Use succinct words to capture the reader's interest.

4. Minimize rambling and be comprehensive and succinct.

5. Make use of capital and lowercase characters. It's simpler to read. Prevent "Shouting," which is written in all capital characters.

6. Steer clear of offensive and harsh language.

7. Don't overload your communication with files.

8. If the email platform permits it, constantly include the name. One's address, which includes one's name, represents a person more accurately than their email address does.

9. Before submitting the email, go over it again and proofread it.

10. Make sure the email is clear of grammar errors and employ spell check to verify proper spelling.

SMS

The ability to transmit and receive textual messages from and to portable devices is known as SMS. Short textual message exchange between mobile handsets is made possible via the SMS communication system. 2.4 billion active customers, or 74 percent of all smartphone users, utilize SMS textual messages as their primary method of information communication, making it the most popular data app in the world. The content could be expressed as a string of letters, figures, or both. Regardless if a data or voice call is currently in place, a portable device that is in use can send or receive a brief message using SMS at any time

Advantages

- A message may be transmitted at any moment,
- it is useful in an emergency, and
- it preserves both money and effort.

Disadvantages

- Extremely brief words or lines can occasionally be misunderstood by the recipient.
- Network congestion causes a lag in the text's transmission.

Teleconference

Teleconferencing is the digital exchange of messages involving two or more individuals in different places. It can be described in its most basic form as the long-available teleconference call. The number of users can indeed be significantly expanded if speakerphones are installed in every workplace. All parties can communicate with each other when employing two-way communication. Oral messages, such as announcements from a corporate president, are conveyed concurrently to numerous places during one-way communication conversations.

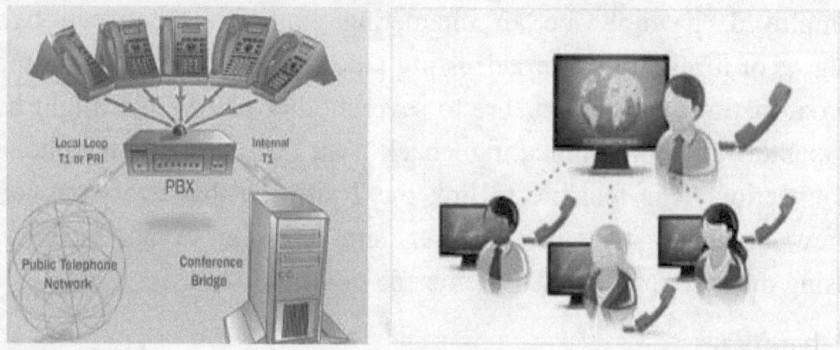

Figure 13: Teleconferencing

Merits

1. Simple to utilize

2. It's simple to get.

3. Simple to take part over any mobile connection in the globe.

4. Setting up a meeting room takes only a short amount of time.

5. Time, money, and resources are saved.

Demerits

The fact that F2F communication between individuals cannot be replaced by teleconferencing is a significant drawback. Teleconferencing won't be effective when individuals would rather connect in person.

Videoconferencing

An ongoing video chat involving two or more people, or involving two or more places. Individuals in distant places can view and hear one another simultaneously through videoconferencing. It is entirely interactive and resembles F2F discussions in many ways. Based on the number of technologies employed, it might be an interacting connection between two places or it might be a broadcasting video, where the site doing the broadcasting sends its picture to several other places that might be capable of communicating back via a regular telephone connection. It is feasible to link the 2 sites so that everyone can view and understand one another, simulating an actual meeting, using more sophisticated systems and devices.

Advantages

1. It replaces direct communication between people.

2. Real-time communication.

3. It solves distance-related obstacles.

4. It results in reduced executive traveling expenses.

5. It results in time savings for conferences.

6. It enables individuals seated in various locations to quickly expand their expertise.

Disadvantages

1. The individual the one wish to speak to must possess the electronic and conferencing-specific gear and software.

2. A computer cannot be carried about like a mobile phone. Consequently, it has an impact on how portable the conferencing performs.

3. A videoconference's confidentiality is not often ensured.

Chapter-3

Information and Communication Technology

The Advancement of Communication and Technology

We identify 5 significant turning points in the history of communication:

- Owing to the development of writing, individuals are now capable to document occurrences and communicate;
- Mass-produced textual materials were made possible with the invention of printing in the 15th century, which allowed for the massive manufacturing of textbooks and other textual materials. Several important societal transformations were carried about by this, such as the rise of newspapers and the expansion of reading and education;
- Instant person-to-person (P2P) interaction by electric power implies - due to the creation of the electro telegraph and the use of Morse protocol by telegraph workers, individuals could converse instantaneously at a range. This made it possible for the telephone to be created later;
- Instant mass media allowed for continuous broadcasting to a large population due to the invention of the radio and subsequently TV; and
- communication made possible by technological advancements involving numerous, concurrent receivers and senders. Computers and individuals today interact with one another as well as with one another with computers.

The application of science

New technologies can be produced by, using scientific concepts in a novel way.

- Numerous variables, such as those listed below, will determine if this technology becomes a well-known product.
- the usefulness of the technology. The silicon chip, for instance, was conceptualized by two independent study groups until it was feasible to manufacture. As they contested who came up with the concept initially, this constituted a windfall for the patent attorneys;
- if the society is prepared to absorb the novel technologies on a societal, political, and economical level. Several societal and economic variables led to the IBM PC's commercial success and its victory over technologically better rivals.

Brian Winston provides a further in-depth evaluation of these procedures. The initial decades of computational development in the later 1940s and early 1950s appear to have been a very stunning period of technical advancement at first glance. However, Winston claims that these devices' transformative power has been, severely muted. For instance:

- The transistor might have been used to create little devices much earlier (some have been, yet they had no real influence).
- The early computers were extremely hard to use and tough to acquire. Certain members of the "old guard" prevented programming language advancement.
- Ancient machines were mostly unimportant to business and trade. Just a handful of businesses recognized the true power.

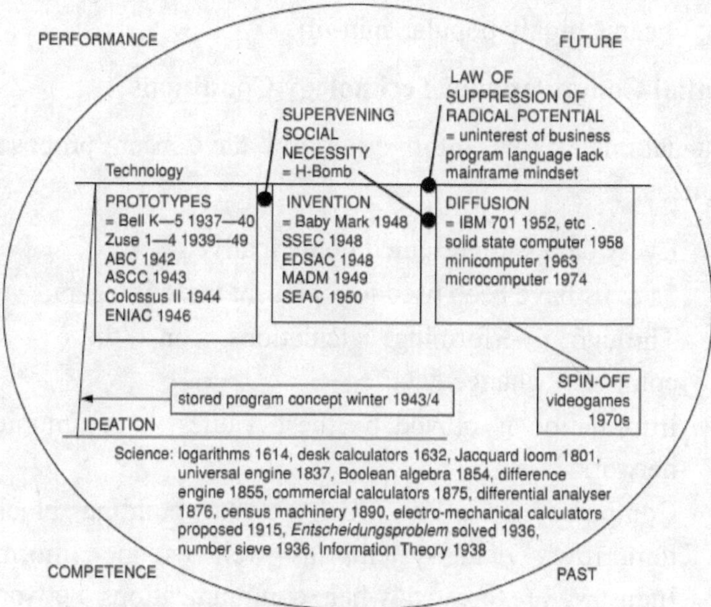

Figure 14: Winston's paradigm illustrates barriers to novel technology adoption

These restraints are depicted in Figure 14 using Winston's paradigm. If models develop into finished products relies on what he refers to as a "supervening societal imperative." If novel technologies are adopted, it will depend on how these societal factors interact. A specific set of societal factors plays a significant role in acting as a "brake" for technical advancement. The "rule of the repression of radical power" is what he refers to as. These limitations guarantee that it would require time for any novel technologies to gain widespread adoption. The lag can be the result of active opposition by societal institutions.

Which has been touted as the electronic substitute for the music cassette? It could collapse until the innovation is in full-level manufacturing (possibly via redundancies). Spin-offs could also result from a novel technique; for instance, the CD has been originally intended to be a product for computer storage; the sound CD has been a highly popular spin-off.

Essential Computational Technology Conditions

5 foundations of the Information Era have been proposed by Dertouzos:

- Every data is represented numerically.
- 1s & 0s have been used to represent these integers.
- Through performing, calculations on these values, computers change data.
- Information is moved by these values in communication networks.
- Computer networks, which are the building blocks of tomorrow's data systems as well as the Information Industry, are created when communications networks & computers operate together.

It is important to go into further depth about certain of these issues. Dertouzos's next claim, for instance, is that since computers utilize binary coding, it is possible to express figures employing the shift, which is the basic electrical connection. As a result, an electrical circuit (a collection of switching) can retain data and do computations. But during the previous 40 years, these circuits have undergone significant technical advancements: they have increased in strength, cost, and size. The valve or suction tubes of the 1950s have given way to a series of microprocessor generations.

What do People do Now that the Tech has Shifted? and how do People keep Generating Revenue?

In the last ten years, CD-ROM encyclopaedias have replaced their paper counterparts, attributed in large part to Microsoft's Encarta, which debuted at a cost that was far lower than that of its printed rivals. Encyclopaedia Britannica, the established industry leader, was significantly impacted by this upheaval, which essentially forced a restructure of the business and its prior sales strategies. After transferring its product to a CD-ROM, the company went one step beyond in 1999 & provided open access to the entire encyclopaedia online over the World Wide Web.

The long-term effects of MP3, which has developed into a convention for storing audio files in computer mode, were the subject of much speculation as we were wrapping off this section in late 2000. Will all album labels be compelled to offer their songs for download on the Internet so that consumers can listen to them on compact MP3 players? Or would this downloading be limited to specific musical genres or target markets? What will the adjustments mean for the traditional album store distribution network?

When it appeared to choose "in 1 step" to redesign all of its key goods to take advantage of the Web, Microsoft has occasionally been described as a firm that "transformed instantly." It's tempting to imagine what would have occurred if it hadn't moved quickly to take advantage of the rise in Internet usage. What occurred is less dramatic.

IT Could Revolutionize a Business

The British nationwide newspaper sector in the late 1980s constituted one striking illustration of this shift. All of the British nationwide newspapers have been written & printed in a confined space in London at the beginning of 1986, near Fleet Square. By the beginning of 1989, they were all relocated and made computers a key component of how they produced newspapers.

All of the major magazines in the country were still using mechanical innovation in the 1970s, which hadn't advanced significantly since the turn of the era. The journalist would initially write up his or her remarks, which would then be converted into rows of lead sorted by a compositor using a Linotype device. Then another group of workers would combine this kind into sheets.

Newspapers are undoubtedly a distinctive product in several respects. They must sell advertising to make money as their covering cost does not contain any profitability margin. A newspaper may have a respectable number of readers but still, experience financial failure if it cannot draw in enough advertisements. Every-day newspapers also only have an extremely short shelf life; if they are not sold on the designated day, they are no longer marketable. Therefore, any lag in bringing the goods to the marketplace has an extremely negative economical impact. This was one of the factors contributing to the industrial unions' significant negotiating impact.

Rupert Murdoch's opening of modern facilities at Wapping in 1986 marked a pivotal development that included several significant technologies:

- **modern technology:** a US news media computer system was utilized in the new factory;
- **novel labour:** Under the terms of a unified union contract, Murdoch hired an entirely novel team to manage the printing part of the business;
- **It switched to a novel distribution** method, using the roads instead of the railroads.

Interestingly, the computer system has been not the finest sophisticated one out there. But after he demonstrated that reliable computer production of national newspapers was possible, additional newspaper organizations quickly followed. This paved the way for the late 1980s & early 1990s to see significantly more sophisticated computer applications.

Industrial activity followed this abrupt upheaval, particularly in the Wapping area. Considering the size of the redundancy, this was not altogether unexpected. The Sunday and daily express, for instance, were the final publications to depart Fleet Square in

November 1989. Just 25 percent of the personnel for these newspapers remained by December of that year.

This instance so exemplifies a number of the traits covered previously in this section:

- Operations can be streamlined and integrated with the help of computer technologies.
- Distant sites can cooperate using a computer and communications technology.
- The introduction of computer technologies could entirely replace conventional operations and artisan capabilities while requiring a novel collection of talents.

The significance of societal and political elements is further highlighted by this instance of research. The influence of the unions was one of the main concerns for owners of national publications. This was far less of a problem for regional newspapers, and the novel technologies have been embraced much extra swiftly and with considerably less friction.

From ...	the wave was ...	characterized by ...
Up to the late 1960s and early 1970s	'The back office (automated accountants)'	Large mainframe systems, using databases to automate functions such as payroll and accounts
The late 1970s and through the 1980s	'The front office (knowledge workers)'	The PC, enabling office workers to handle document production, spreadsheets, etc. for themselves
The arrival of the Internet and Web in 1994	'The virtual office (the global marketplace)'	The move to networking for organizations of all sizes

Figure 15: IT advancements inside business contexts

The Transition from IT to ICT

The integration of the Online & the WWW is typically the foundation for the "data superhighway" concept that has captivated certain computer experts, not to note influential governmental people. Despite they are occasionally confused, these were not identical items. A network of networks (N2N) is the simplest way to describe the Online. It is the network of digital links that allows people to transmit and access data in different manners. The WWW, which we will henceforth refer to as the Web, is one among these methods.

From a modest network of US army and academic locations in the early 1960s, the Internet has expanded into a global N2N that shares a framework of protocols for sending and receiving content. For instance, "Http" refers to Hypertext Transfer Protocol, a collection of protocols that enables the communication between networks and particular devices as well as the retrieval of documents from and uploading to websites.

Fundamentally described, a server is a machine that stores data that may be shared through a network and the Web. Various things are possible thanks to other protocols. FTP, for instance, enables you to download a file onto the computer from a distant computer.

We are now able to converse in manners that seemed like science fiction just a couple of generations ago because of technology. For instance, with the home PC and the appropriate tools and connectivity, one can:

- connect to other computers anywhere in the globe in a few of mins, while this timeline is frequently overly optimistic during peak moments;
- download data from computers all around the globe;
- send and receive emails from individuals worldwide;
- peruse the data available in libraries and colleges around the world;
- Search databases worldwide;
- engage in online gaming involving players from around the globe;

- make the database publicly available such that anyone in the globe might conceivably access it;
- retrieve and replay multimedia files, including video and audio recordings.

All of these resources are also accessible to any business, regardless of size. Additionally, business consumers can currently transact business online by selling commodities and activities (a practice known as e-commerce, which we'll discuss subsequently). For a while now, these services have indeed been accessible via the Internet. Yet these developments are based on several really old concepts.

E-commerce

The electronic road is not just available for business; it is moving, reconstructing, and reshaping businesses in America, according to Mary Cronin, who wrote one of the original textbooks to examine the prospective users of the Web to business. Although e-commerce has increased, it has not yet reached the levels suggested, perhaps due to financial prudence. According to this statement, "only as dependable transit and safe cash are essential to commercial activity in the material realm, so safety and digital transactions devices would then be at the core of e-commerce." Recent software developments do appear to have overcome these transaction and safety concerns. We anticipate significant growth shortly.

As evidenced by the expanding media emphasis in publications, periodicals, and tv, there is undoubtedly increased enthusiasm for making purchases through the Internet. One significant consequence is that smaller businesses can afford to use these technologies. Comparing the price of launching and maintaining a tiny website against the price of traditional global marketing. M In fact, more than just Web software is required to maintain a profitable website on the Internet. The next items are recommended by PC Magazine for setting up the facilities:

- a web server or computer used to host a website;
- Web server program for the creation and upkeep of the website;
- merchant gateway program, which lets clients purchase their goods online;
- transaction software that makes it possible for customers to make secure payments;
- ancillary software to handle additional data and tasks like shipment, taxation, and so forth.;
- a safety "security system" (software that guards your business network against viruses and hackers);
- a fast internet or phone connectivity.

A smaller business is not required to invest in this system. It could establish an online appearance at a reasonable expense by utilizing service providers to offer network connectivity and security software.

The increase in online marketing is another sign of the expansion of commerce via the Internet. We might also draw attention to the rapid development of the Internet alone. Radio required 38 years, tv 13, cable TV 10, and online just 5 years to achieve 50 million viewers.

Certain businesses are already utilizing the Online in a pretty innovative manner to assist all kinds of economic activities. For instance, a lot of big businesses are progressively adopting Online for hire. It might be necessary for candidates to upload their CVs digitally, and that material might then be verified digitally. To create a profile, candidates might also be required to undergo a lengthy and in-depth online survey. At this point, applicants with undesirable profiles might be dropped.

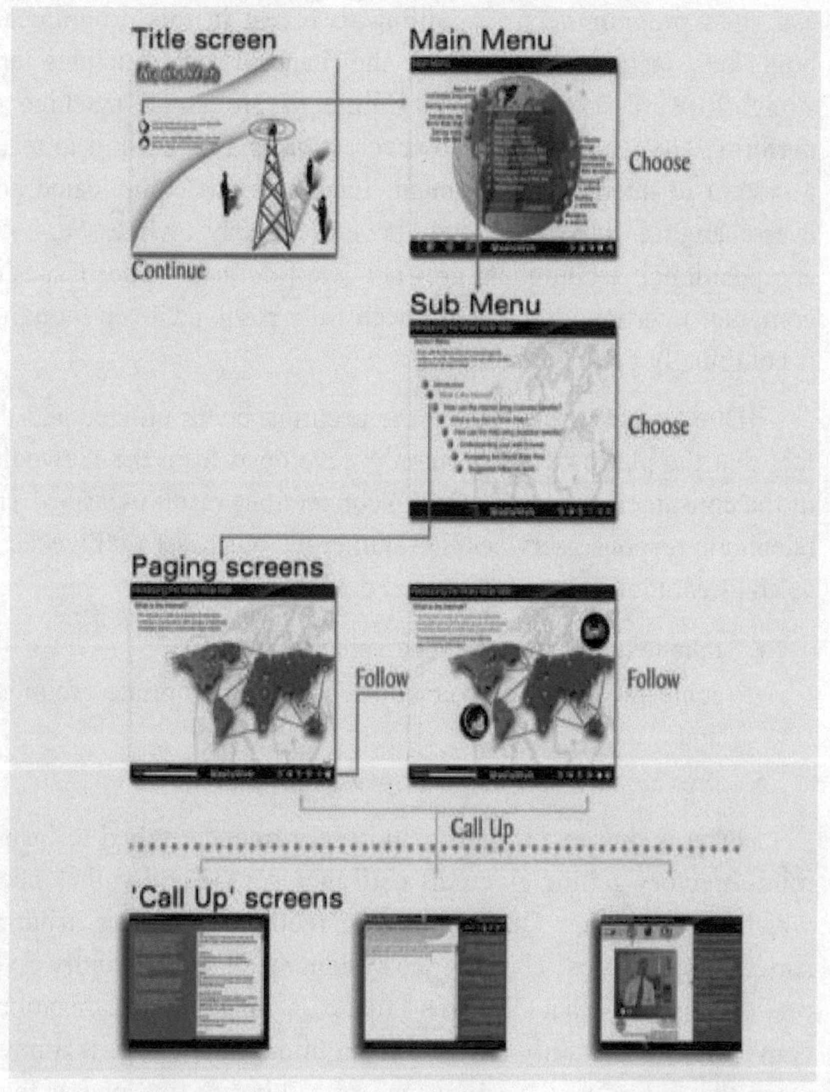

Figure 16: Hypermedia Utilization in CD-ROM Projects

ICT Applications Communication Issues

Human-to-computer (H2C) as well as computer-to-computer (C2C) interaction, as we just established, are characteristics of ICT. A program controls how efficiently a system can process data and communicate. The ability of developers and the amount of cash that programmers are willing to invest in this program are both key factors. In light of the handful of principles and straightforward methods, it is simple to program a machine to perform zeros and crosses. However, it takes a lot of skill to teach a system to interpret a document. Language has complicated and ever-changing laws, as we have previously witnessed, and compositional techniques are not well-defined. The issue of computer interpretation has not been fully resolved, even though it is continually getting better.

Due to the constraints of the program being utilized and the fact that the platform is not mainly developed from the viewpoint of the consumer, numerous (H2C) connections result in issues. The telephone response services that numerous businesses utilize serve as an illustration. These automated devices are made to

- take texts for missing receivers,
- route incoming conversations to the appropriate recipient, and
- provide any data that the speaker might require.

Data is presented tightly, and users frequently had to hear a mini-directory getting given off until they get the option they need, which causes issues. One can also be required to endure irritating songs and messages. The way the system responds frequently gives off the sense that it was made with the organization's convenience—certainly not yours—in mind. Phone rage is a novel word that refers to the annoyance of talking on the phone for a long time without speaking to anyone. This is a straight result of attempting to interact with a computer whose reaction options are extremely constrained and rigid. Since numerous of these applications flout norms for effective communication, organizations must think extremely hard before implementing them.

Of course, more advanced voice identification technologies, which promise to enable systems to "recognize, comprehend, and react to typical human discourse," might substitute these technologies in the future. So instead of needing to utilize limited orders or reactions or input certain keystrokes on the phone dial, voice identification technologies must enable one to inquire for the data you require in your usual conversational tone.

Despite significant advancements in the last ten years, voice identification software still struggles to handle less predictable language. Personalized dictating into a PC is improving, even though there are nevertheless significant obstacles.

For automation and digital systems in businesses, there are other crucial challenges. Initially, there can be problems with accountability and responsibility. When correspondence served as the primary method of conducting business, there have been frequently quite tight laws governing how this must be accomplished. These regulations included things like how messages were saved and recorded, who may sign which types of messages, and how the correspondence has been examined. Of course, email allows you to accomplish all of these tasks, yet numerous companies don't appear to have the appropriate infrastructure in place. There are also safety concerns. Further instances of how computer technologies have collapsed due to inadequate consideration of human processes.

Unit-III

Correspondence on Recruitment

Chapter- 1

Employment Applications and Resume Development

Application Letters

For positions that are open in corporations or governmental agencies, applications are frequently requested. In reaction to an ad or as a self-initiated proposition, application letters are referred to as soliciting or unsolicited letters, accordingly.

A cover letter, also known as an application letter, should always be included alongside a candidate's resume to inform the reader of what candidates are submitting, why candidates are submitting it, and how they will profit from viewing it. As everyone has a certain role to play, the applicant should always submit their resume and cover letter jointly. One's CV should pique potential employers' curiosity to request an interview. Getting companies intrigued sufficiently to view their resume is the goal of their application letter.

- Applications for a Position: Date and applicant's location.
- The employer's or business's identity and complete location.
- Salutation.
- The application's body.
  - The opening paragraph.
  - The paragraph's description of the candidate.
  - The final paragraph.
- Complimentary application ends.
- The applicant's signature.

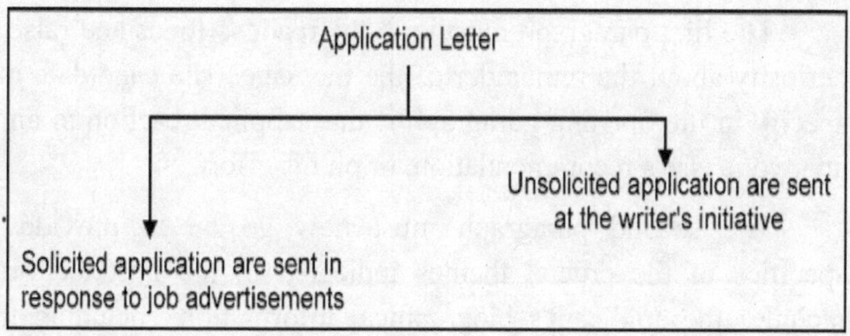

Figure 17: Application letter

Solicited Letters

When applicants apply for a position that has been posted or in response to an employment advertisement, they must include a requested cover letter. Introduce oneself and the reason for the letter's existence in the beginning. For instance, "I am writing, regarding the available marketing manager role applicant have listed on the company website. You can see from my accompanying résumé that I have ten years of communications and marketing expertise and have held a range of positions for both major and medium-sized organizations ".

Unsolicited Letters

An unsolicited application letter is intended to introduce oneself to a prospective employer, perhaps for a position that is currently open, or to learn more about an organization you are interested in working for. The former is referred to as "prospecting" and is employed to introduce yourself and the type of position you are seeking to an employer. The letter must include an introduction to you, a list of your qualifications, and a succinct statement as to the reason you are writing. Make a note of reasons you believe you would be a suitable fit for the organization for either a current position or a prospective position.

Body of the Application

The first paragraph must grab the reader's focus and raise his curiosity about the remainder of the message. The candidate must specify in the opening paragraph if they applied reaction to an ad, at anyone else's recommendation, or on his effort.

The second paragraph must now go on to provide the specifics of the crucial themes indicated in the introduction. It includes the applicant's biographical information, including their age, marital position, academic background, work history, and languages they are fluent in, among other things. If references are requested, they can be provided including complete addresses in a different paragraph.

Applications shouldn't include undesirable information such as household issues, expenditures for the household, and so on. Never mention the current employer negatively while applying for positions with higher opportunities.

An applicant must state in the conclusion that they would assist the company to the extent of its capabilities and that they will complete his obligations to the complete contentment of the employer.

Letters General Notes

- The candidate's address and contact information are provided in the letter's upper-right corner.

- A clean design is required; the optimal configuration is a customized frame or semi-block.

- The cover letter must indeed be properly handwritten in the ink of dark blue or ballpoint pen if the ad specifies that the application should be handwritten in the participant's handwriting.

- Use the address listed in the advertising when addressing the letter. The salutation should be "Sirs" if the letter is going to be addressed to a business. When writing to a specific person, use the salutation "Sir." Yours faithfully is the proper closing for an application.

- Applications never include original paperwork, such as certifications. There are just authorized versions included. At the interview, authentic records are presented. Any of the below papers might be used as the initial step of an application:

- I am interested in applying for the Systems Administrator position at the company that was posted on March 22 in the "Indian Express."

- I would like to be taken into consideration for the position of Account Manager at the company, which, as I comprehend it, has become open.

- In regards to the ad from the "Times of India" on September 25, 2007. I submit my application for your company's position of the desktop operator.

The candidate might feel free to add one of the accompanying lines to the conclusion.

- I am writing this with the hope that my background and expertise will be worthy of your attention.

- The possibility of a successful career comes before money.

- I eagerly await the chance to conduct a job interview with you.

Application Letters Mistakes

Ensure you avoid making any of the below mistakes. While certain of these errors are quite apparent, others are simpler to overlook. Yet they all share the same trait—you must stay away from them at all expenses!

➤ Leaving your cover letter without a signature.

- ➢ Incorporating personal data that is unrelated to the position you're seeking: I've been unemployed for 8 months, and I require this employment.
- ➢ Providing information about oneself is more appropriate for a dating site rather than employment "Catholic, single guy who likes to jump in their free time."
- ➢ Inconsistent business data; the letter is addressed to Star Organization yet references Moon Insurance.
- ➢ Grease or foodstuff spots might be seen on the sheet or envelope.
- ➢ The names are misspelled.
- ➢ The cover letter should be handwritten, not typed. Except when handwritten cover letters are desired.
- ➢ Losing your resume in the mail.
- ➢ Terrible corrections
- ➢ The cover letter is more difficult to attach by stapling than by clipping.
- ➢ Rejecting a wage criteria demand when the job posting requests it. If possible, give a spectrum rather than a precise number.

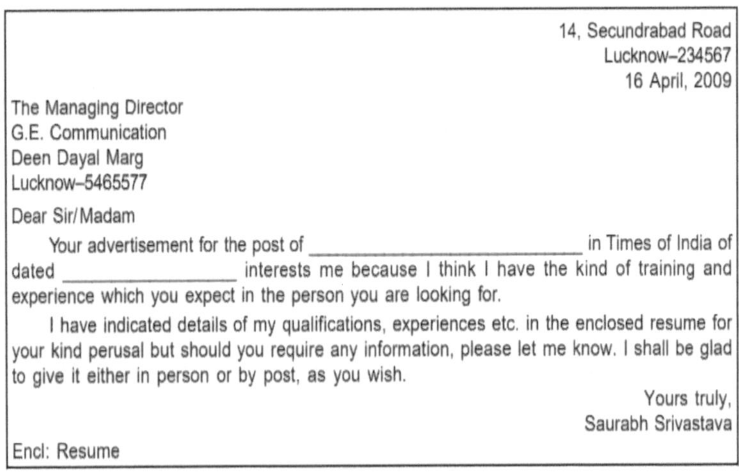

14, Secundrabad Road
Lucknow–234567
16 April, 2009

The Managing Director
G.E. Communication
Deen Dayal Marg
Lucknow–5465577

Dear Sir/Madam

Your advertisement for the post of ___________________________ in Times of India of dated ________________ interests me because I think I have the kind of training and experience which you expect in the person you are looking for.

I have indicated details of my qualifications, experiences etc. in the enclosed resume for your kind perusal but should you require any information, please let me know. I shall be glad to give it either in person or by post, as you wish.

Yours truly,
Saurabh Srivastava

Encl: Resume

Figure 18: Example of application letter

Application Letters Checklist

To be certain candidates have not overlooked something crucial, answer oneself the accompanying 10 queries.

- ➤ Have I checked my letter at minimum twice for typographic, grammatical, and grammatical errors?
- ➤ Is there a particular recipient listed on the letter? Have I written the people's names properly and included their exact titles?
- ➤ Is my signature in black or blue ink on the letter?
- ➤ Is the length of my message limited to one sheet and 3 to 5 brief paragraphs?
- ➤ Have I used key points to underline my strong points in the 2nd or 3rd paragraph?
- ➤ Is the application letter written with the employer's needs in mind rather than with my demands—like cash or flexibility hours mind?
- ➤ Do I possess a version of the application letter for personal files?
- ➤ Have I provided my compensation data if it was requested particularly? (If it was not requested, you should not indicate your compensation.)
- ➤ Do I have my resume with me? Have I carefully wrapped it into 3rd and tucked it beneath the application letter without using staples so that it will fit inside a regular-sized envelope?
- ➤ Have I signed my signature in black or blue ink since that's the significant thing individuals neglect to do?

Resume

A resume describes a person's educational history, professional experience, and anticipated professional path. A resume is an organized, written description of an individual's training, experience, and job credentials. The CV-Curriculum

Vitae is indeed the main tool you can use to introduce yourself to a potential employer as an employment applicant. However, a large number of job searchers do not take the necessary time and care to appropriately prepare their CVs. As a consequence, many would-be employees miss out on the chance to promote themselves and demonstrate their capabilities during job interviews.

Purpose

1. Complete the employer's assessment procedure (minimum academic requirement, number of years of experience, and so forth.).

2. Include a current address and phone contact information (one that would constantly be manned during business sessions) as well as contact details.

Resume Types

Create a résumé that is functional, chronological or both. The candidate's objectives and the background will determine the best option.

❖ **Chronological**

Following the name, residence, and optional goals, the job experience part takes over and is positioned in the position with the highest visibility. You create this part by systematically stating your employment in reverse chronological sequence, starting with your latest post and moving backward toward older employment. Providing the greatest room to the most latest post, briefly discuss your duties and achievements beneath every category. This chronological method can indeed be changed if you have recently graduated from university and have little to no work expertise. Doing so will draw focus to your academic background.

❖ **Functional**

Highlight your abilities and skills by listing employment and educational qualifications in the latter parts. This format is occasionally referred to as a competent résumé. This style emphasizes certain competencies, making it helpful for those who are simply starting their professions, want to change directions in their jobs, or have minimal consistent work-related experience.

❖ **Combination**

Try using a hybrid resume to emphasize your talents while still giving a chronological background of your career if you do not possess a lot of employment experience to list.

Preparing for Creating a Resume

❖ An employer typically gives a CV no greater than 30 secs of attention. A CV must be accurate and understandable. Data that is unneeded or useless must be eliminated.

❖ An applicant with little or no expertise must not have a CV that is more than 1 or 2 pages.

❖ The best method to market oneself is with a CV. It must thus be appealing. However, color printing or paper shouldn't be utilized for this. You could bold, italicize, or underline text to draw attention to it.

❖ Keep in note that a potential employer would judge you negatively if your resume has any form of spelling or grammar error. It would convey the appearance that you are unable to complete any tasks properly.

❖ As a result, after creating the candidate's CV, carefully read it before having who is familiar with proper English examine it.

❖ Attempt to modify your CV to the employment needs when submitting for a specific job posting. You must attentively study the job posting and conduct a study about it. You might describe the locations you have visited and remained at if, for instance, you are aware that the company can place the position anyplace in Bangladesh. If the employer is seeking an organizer, you might once more emphasize the organizing projects you worked on while a student. It would add to the worth of your resume.

❖ It is crucial that you provide accurate and factual data on your CV. In a job interview, you shouldn't provide any data that might be perceived as false.

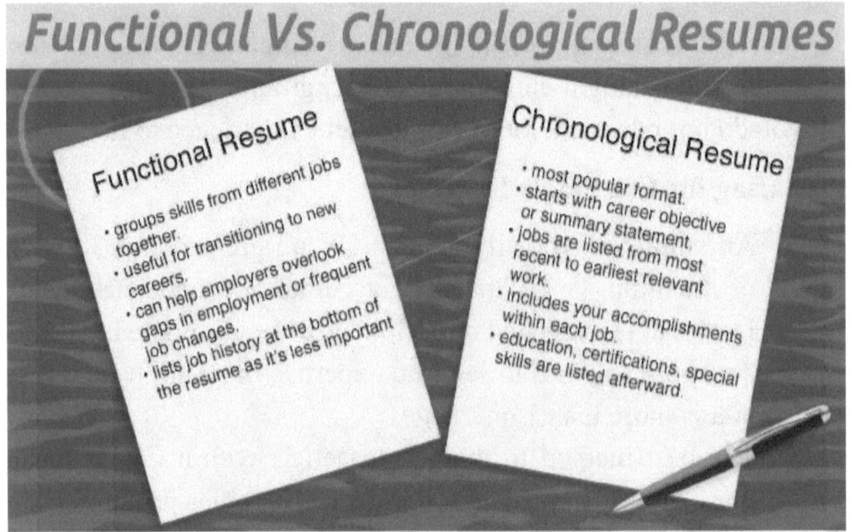

Figure 19: Chronological and functional resume

Resume Parts

A systematic presentation of the essential details is required for a CV:

➢ Title
➢ Career summaries are most useful for people with experience.
➢ The majority of new candidates should use a career aim.
➢ Experience
➢ Additional Details

> Education
> References
> Personal Details

Title

The title would start with the name. It ought to be in bold and large font size (do not add any nickname). After that, include personal contact information, including phone number & email address, at one's current mailing address. To grab readers' focus, this section would be placed in the page's midsection.

Summary of the Career

This applies primarily to people with experience of at least 4-5 years. In no more than six to seven lines, describe the areas of candidate experience. Describe the candidate's career accomplishments in a few words (if any).

Aim of the Career

Typically speaking, applicants who are new to the job market or who have limited expertise (1- 2 years) should read this part. In this section, describe the candidate's career's short-term objective. Be sure to describe how your qualifications and prospects fit the job for which you are applying. Promote your advantageous job-related talents. It's crucial to tailor your career objective to the requirements listed in the job posting. Place a strong emphasis on how you could contribute to the firm and what you want from it.

Experience

This part ought to appear before the part on academic qualifications for qualified applicants.

The following are elements to include in the applicant's experience specifics:

> Name of Organization
> Designation

> Dates from and to
> Work commitment
> Special Accomplishment

If the applicant has experience operating in multiple roles within the same company, describe it in stages.

Give a summary of your latest encounter initially, and then list each of your previous encounters in reverse chronological sequence, with your earliest experience coming to a close. It is preferable to keep quiet about brief and inconsequential experiences. Avoid having a significant time difference between employment.

Qualification of Education

For a new employee, the education and training component must arrive before the expertise component. You will provide the accompanying details with your mention of your educational credentials.

> Degree's name
> Duration
> Board and organization names.
> Examination year and the day the results were published (if needed),
> Results and accomplishments

As with the expertise portion, you should start by mentioning the applicant's most current degree before moving on to the others one at a time. Keep in mind that it appears strange to discuss the outcome of one degree while avoiding another.

You could include any training programs you have taken or participated in that complement your professional expertise. Specify the training facility, the subject, and the length of the training. The category of training might come just after the section on schooling.

Additional Details

The data that does not fit in the previously mentioned portions yet is connected to the employment displayed in this section. For instance:

> Professional Success
> Award
> linguistic ability
> computational expertise
> publications, a license, and governmental identification.
> volunteering, and so on.

Personal Details

In this part candidates' present and permanent address, contact number, blood group, religion, hobby, etc. can be mentioned.

Reference

Any name of family relations must not be listed as a referral in the reference section. Referrals ought to be individuals who have observed the applicant closely during your time as a student or employee. You should include the referral's name, contact information, and email address, if applicable. It is preferable to list 2 or 3 referrals. It is crucial to let the applicant referral know that applicant listed him in the applicant's CV as a reference.

Figure 20: Guidelines for Writing Resume

Guidelines for Writing Resume

The applicant just has a bit over 30 secs to establish a strong first impact when an interviewer goes through their CV. That is often how long recruiters take to peruse a resume. One must be concise and precise to keep the reader's interest, yet that is not everything. The accompanying pointers should be kept in consideration when writing a resume:

> ➢ Recruiters are not interested in reading a lengthy, detailed account of life's achievements. They possess a tone of resumes to go through and need to decide promptly if you will be a suitable match for their organization. So, be succinct and demonstrate your expertise. Just data that would persuade a potential recruiter to interview you must be included on a resume. The statements of pertinent abilities and feats ought to be succinct and direct. Long statements and expertise that aren't related would obscure the key details. Incorporate personal details only when it clearly illustrates an essential aspect of your personality. A CV must only highlight your abilities at work, not in your free time.

> ➢ Set up your professional goal before you start creating the resume. Get it concise and targeted. Once you list essential talents and highlight professional strengths in the resume, remember to maintain consistency in the messaging.

> ➢ A Professional Goal section ought to be included at the start of the resume if you are the latest graduate or possess little work history. This would assist draw the reader's interest in you and define the kind of employment you are seeking. If you possess expertise in the area of work, you should include a strong Concise summary at the start of the resume that highlights the finest credentials for the job. A strong introduction must persuade a potential reader to continue reading.

- Utilize professional terminology and acronyms to show that you are knowledgeable about the employer's sector, yet not to the stage that it becomes difficult to read or comprehend your resume. If an acronym, like TQM-Total Quality Management, is not immediately apparent, please define it in parentheses.
- Explain your experiences in terms of the abilities the recruiter is looking for. Emphasize achievements that would catch the attention of recruiters who are reading the CV. How could this applicant succeed in the position and have a good influence? If a corporation is seeking an employee with leadership potential, emphasize your background in project management or novel hire training. Recall that getting the interview is the main objective.
- Use descriptive keywords on the resume to raise the notice of your qualifications. As more employers scan for applications in computerized databases that discover similarities based on keywords, it's critical to include relevant keywords in the resume. These phrases must showcase your skill level while relating to the position you are looking for.
- The greatest resumes include action-pre lines, which highlight a decision you made in reaction to a problem or a chance and indicate why it benefited your employer. This approach shows why you can succeed and get outcomes while bringing your expertise lines to existence. "Investigated dropping revenue and devised advertising that boosted sales over 30 percent in less than one month," can be an example of an action-pro claim. This sentence enumerates the circumstances or problems you encountered (falling revenues), the measure you made (creating a promotion), as well as the result of your activities (a 30% rise in sales).

- One must provide the readers a sense of things you have accomplished during your employment, yet rather than concentrating on the responsibilities you held at your most recent positions, mention your achievements in action-pro lines containing quantitative data to support your assertions. To demonstrate your achievement in attaining corporate objectives, utilize figures, ratios, and cash figures. Employ "Sales increase in the area 150 percent during 6 months" in place of "Responsible for raising revenues in my area."

- Project an image of yourself as someone who is engaged, successful, smart, and ready to contribute. Instances include "organized," "established," "developed," "managed," "created," "structured," and "supervised." Avoid using a similar action term more than once. Use a thesaurus and seek professional guidance If you are experiencing trouble thinking of different methods to convey a similar thing, examine web pages and other resources.

- Why fill up important areas on your resume with material irrelevant to the employment you're applying for when you do not have enough room? Never discuss personal matters like religion, gender, marital background, age, politics, or perhaps personal ideas; instead, concentrate on your professional achievements. It would be unlawful for employers to take such matters into consideration in all but limited circumstances. Resist using comedy and clichés in your resumes, and don't state that you like to surf and watch horror films in your free time.

- Instead of only putting personal qualities like "Reliable, Well Structured, Self-Motivated, and Professional" on your resume, try presenting instances from your experiences to illustrate these qualities. For instance, write "Did not ever miss an essential deadline in 5 yrs. as a project leader" rather than "Reliable."

➢ Your resume must give the best impression of who you are. If you lack any of the skills a potential company is looking for, do not draw attention to them. Consider what you could contribute.

➢ Exaggerating or misrepresenting your knowledge and capabilities can only make matters worse.

➢ Recruiters look at the resume for expertise to determine how well-organized, reasonable, and precise you are. Ensure the resume is coherent, well-balanced, tidy, and eye-catching. Section titles should stand out and be properly separated from one another.

➢ Give up using extravagant, wonderful vocabulary. In other terms, avoid attempting to attract potential recruiters with an extensive vocabulary. Employ language that is clear to all.

➢ To make the cv extra compact, attempt to group any brief parts. If you just possess a single-entry under-employment, for instance, you might want to move it underneath education and rename the category "Education and Training."

Figure 21: Resume exteriors

Resume Exteriors

- A resume must be as comprehensive as necessary to include all of your greatest and most pertinent skills for the position you're applying for. You ought to be capable to fit the whole of your pertinent expertise on one page for fresh grads or those having just a couple of years of expertise. A two-page resume can be necessary to highlight all of your pertinent accomplishments if you possess a lot of prior experience in your profession. The content on your resume should be pertinent to the job you are pursuing, and its clarity and conciseness should be prioritized over its size. The length of a cv is not as crucial as if or not it adequately outlines your finest credentials for the position.

- Utilize an offset sheet that is conventional A4 or letters (8 and a half" x 11"). Employers deal with a large volume of applications; if yours appears on a shorter page, it might get misplaced in the stack, and if it is huge, it might get wrinkled and have difficulties getting into a firm's folder.

- The only sheet colors deemed suitable for applications and cover letters are white and ivory.

- Using a laptop or word processing to create the resume offers the most flexibility. You can save various draughts on discs and execute modifications virtually instantaneously as a result. Additionally, word processing programs offer a wide range of options, including justified borders, alternative fonts, bold-facing for prominence, and numerous font families.

- Avoid using a photocopier when making copies and instead, use the highest grade offset printing method you can discover. Your résumé will just be seen by the personnel department; copies will be available to everybody. Versions of copies easily lose their legibility.

> Errors on applications can indeed be humiliating, and when there is one, you will undoubtedly be the only person who loses. So make sure to properly review your application, and then possess a partner to examine it. Ensure your grammar and spelling are flawless. Do not just depend on the built-in spell-check features of word processing or computers since not all typos are spelling errors and a spell checker cannot take the place of checking your application. Even perfectly spelled terms can be misused.

> In the resume body, utilize bulletin points rather than lengthy essays. Everything you could do to pique the reader's interest would help you get an interview because applications are read rather rapidly. Employ a consistent layout for titles and bulletin points and pick typefaces that are simple to read.

> Additionally, be certain to use bolded text or capital letters and to give appropriate space between every part. To draw attention to the content on your application that is most important, employ bold, italicized, and underlining. In a similar vein, until you are applying for a career that requires a lot of creativity, avoid flashy formats or too inventive applications with unique fonts or images. Keep your resume straightforward, confident, and polished.

> It is the equivalent to draw interest to anything and nothing at all. For the greatest impact on the exact locations, you wish to call interest to, employ emphasizing techniques like bold, italicized, and underlining sparingly.

Chapter - 2

Employment Interviews and Correspondences

References

A referee is someone willing to offer other individuals an undertaking. The firm can choose the individuals who are qualified for the job by using the tests and interviews he/she administers. Before sending the appointment letter, he/she might need to learn more regarding the chosen applicant's dependability, sincerity, suitability for the position, and some other facts that may be pertinent.

As a result, it is usually required of candidates to identify in their applications an individual or people who are ready to serve as a trustworthy source of facts regarding them. Keep the below things in mind while addressing a referee:

1. Speak courteously.

2. The message should specifically ask the candidate for details.

3. The letter must be labelled "confidential" to protect confidentiality.

4. It is good to include a stamped, self-addressed letter for the referee's comfort.

5. The referee should guarantee that the details he/she provides would be kept private.

Group discussions

One way to build their original approaches to information is through discussion. People tend to pay attention to individuals in a discussion since they infer and think they can add something useful. They develop the ability to communicate their ideas to others quite clearly. Candidates also get to develop arguments before bringing them to a conclusion.

The act of discussion involves intellect, reflection, and opinions. One might talk about prepared topics for a while in a discussion, yet one can push their preconceived notions. It is reflected since his/her ideas and opinions are influenced by what other people say and feel. Disputes are resolved and equilibrium is achieved through a constructive and effective debate. In a group discussion, every person shares their creative thinking by making suggestions, contributing concepts, and then introducing other concepts with alternative answers till all concepts have indeed been properly listed.

The following are some important characteristics of group discussions:

1. **Communication:** Communication between the different group participants is a fundamental aspect of group discussions. By paying focus to one another, they examine one another and exchange verbal messages.

2. **Group participants:** Just a group of people that includes a leader and members can have a successful group discussion. To solve an issue, the group needs to come to an agreement on solutions, combine the details and information, and simulate reasoning. As they do their assigned tasks, the group participants effectively connect.

3. **Participation:** The efficacy and effectiveness of group discussions are heavily reliant on the attentive contribution of the participants.

4. **Interpersonal attractiveness**: Another distinguishing quality of a group discussion comprises interpersonal attractiveness. Participants' preferences, inclinations, behavior, and disposition are recognizable to one another as long as

the discussion occurs. Empathy grows between individuals, and people share each other's issues as a result.

5. **Stress to follow the norms**: There is constantly a component of stress to follow the norms and standards in a group discussion. The specified and established criteria are constantly maintained and respected

6. **Discrepancy:** It is a dispute, disagreement, or difference between group participants that frequently emerges amid debates and discussions. It could imitate the participants to generate fresh approaches to the issue.

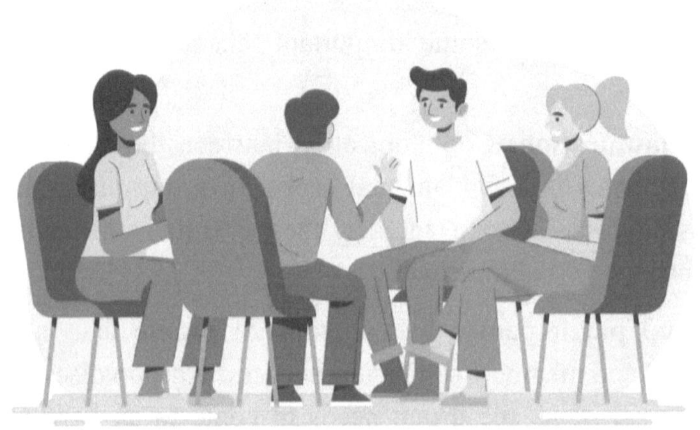

Figure 22: Group discussion

Group discussion factors

1. **Discussion goals:** The major goal of group discussions is to assess how well individuals act in a group. The opportunity to express individual personality attributes, such as intelligence, ingenuity, and problem-solving methods, as well as potential leadership abilities and group dynamics, is provided through group discussions. They evaluate their participation based on the precision of their reasoning and the ease of their communication. In the meantime, individuals also develop

excellent communication skills for their ideas and thoughts. They offer people ways to let go of their prejudicial opinions and refrain from acting in prejudicial ways.

2. **Discussion purpose:** Providing a forum for group education is the group discussion's major purpose. It seeks to open up the possibility of talking about an issue. In a group discussion, the members make an effort to find a solution. They discuss their results while classifying and examining the pre-existing results. Participating in discussion as a technique encourages group thinking. For problem-solving and decision-making, the group engages in collaborative thinking. The purpose of the group discussion is to develop individuals into mature, responsible adults. People discover group dynamics as a result of the easy stream of communication inside the group.

3. **Members in a group discussion:** There must be enough members for an effective group discussion. Nevertheless, it might be challenging to pinpoint the ideal number of players for a discussion to be productive. The number of individuals in one group has an impact on the character and efficiency of the discussion. The recommended number of people in a group for a productive and profitable discussion is 5-9. A fair conversation, on the other hand, can occur when all participants express their perspectives and exchange facts.

4. **Discussion location:** A group discussion must start happening in a well-chosen location. It must be well-ventilated and well-lit. It ought to possess a comfortable ambiance with a circular layout of seats for members so that all members can view one another comfortably and evenly.

The issue must be announced to the members after they have gathered. The individuals are provided 5-10 mins to evaluate their problematic ideas. Another method is to make the issue known in advance, and the conversation will begin when everyone has arrived at the table prepared.

5. **Observer position:** An observer is present during a group discussion. The observer's job is to absorb information and carefully examine the discussion procedure. He/she bears an eye on the attendees and how they interact during the conversation.

Skills for discussion

Individuals must develop their speaking and listening abilities to contribute effectively to a group discussion.

1. **Knowledge of the subject matter:** To have a productive debate, people ought to be able to articulate the areas that call for particular focus and thought. Individuals need to be able to describe, expound, contrast, examine, demonstrate, connect, summarize', and review many topics. With understanding and facts concerning the topic, people ought to be formulated for discussion.

2. **A member must possess a distinctive or remarkable vocal with a nice and entertaining tone.** He/she utters phrases correctly, emphasizing the right accent. The presence of an amazing voice draws in more listeners.

3. **Pronunciation:** Candidates must be capable to vary their voice while speaking clearly and placing emphasis on individual syllables.

4. **Poise:** His/her general demeanour and poise help people keep their composure. Poise prevents people from pronouncing an individual or a particular viewpoint. The traits of poise comprise assurance, brevity, composure, and attention. All of them enable individuals to contribute effectively to a discussion.

5. **Useful body language:** To participate in a debate effectively, people must refrain from making too many gestures or motions of the body while they are speaking. There ought to be no hostility, irritability, tiredness, anxiety, rush, or hesitancy in human body language.

Listener skills

1. **A positive attitude:** To have a fruitful discussion, both the listener and observer should adopt a positive attitude. We give others our whole attention.

2. **A concentrated attitude**: One should keep their thoughts on the topic or the issue being discussed. It enables it simpler to comprehend the specific topic at hand as well as the speaker's intentions.

3. **Systemic perception**: To participate in a discussion effectively, it is important to understand the points of view being discussed. People must examine other people's perspectives and viewpoints logically and impartially. One must pay attention to what others have to express so that one can change their viewpoints in response.

4. **Detailed assessment**: As participants, one must understand how and what to listen for, and how to understand what is being said. One ought to be able to generalize or evaluate the data collected. This must be accomplished by making an accurate comparison between the previous understanding and the newly discovered information.

5. **Body language:** When participating in a discussion, it is important to be open and nice to receive the ideas and views of everyone else. Therefore, we shouldn't make antagonistic gestures. While being open and accommodating, people must also avoid being defensive.

Good discussions helped people come up with ever-newer concepts. By examining the attraction and legitimacy of their ideas, people discover ways to communicate them. Individuals exchange ideas and views in discussions. Our ability to learn is greatly influenced by discussion. We discover the kind of function a group attempt has in the contemporary environment through the procedure of group discussion. People also discover ways to appreciate one another's opinions, collaborate and think critically so that disagreements and misunderstandings are resolved at every stage.

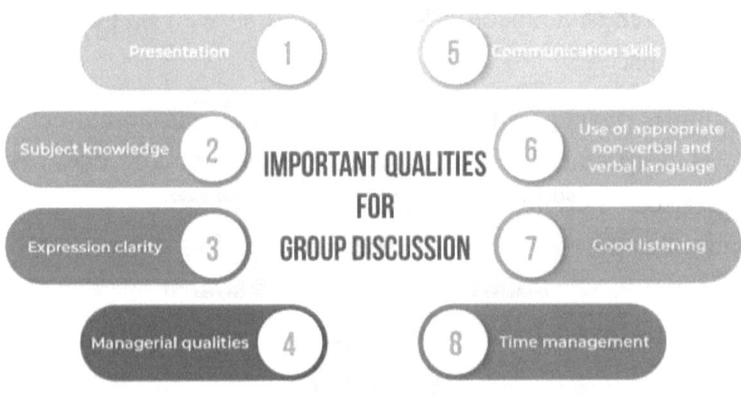

Figure 23: Skills for group discussion

Interview

Interview translates as "perspective between" or "view between." It implies a conversation between 2 individuals to learn more about one another or to learn to know one another. Alternatively, we may state that it represents the communication between the interviewee and the interviewer. A 2-way communication method is an interview.

Recruiters would learn more about your personality, preferences, ambitions, and goals throughout the interview. This is the candidate's chance to provide concrete instances and anecdotes plus describe how this expertise makes you the ideal applicant for the job. You won't just be a collection of abilities and accomplishments on a sheet of paper anymore. The time is right to show that you are interested in the job and that you are knowledgeable about the organization and the sector. Be yourself because this is the moment for the recruiter to get to know you.

Interview types

1. **Promotion interview**: Even when there is no competitive pressure, candidates for promotions are nevertheless questioned. This style of interview is quite casual and acts as an introduction to prospective roles and obligations. Additionally, if there is a contest for promotions, the interview aids in the recruitment procedure and might provide a chance for applicants to explain their professional options.

2. **Evaluation Interview**: One way of routine worker evaluation is the appraisal interview. The ideal technique for evaluating workers' productivity is through a yearly evaluation interview. A F2F, private conversation gives the two of them the chance to converse about a variety of work-related topics. This interview is additionally of a conversation than a question-and-answer session. The evolution of the profession, flaws, regions that require development, instruction, prospects for advancement, etc. is the main topics.

3. **Leave interview**: A worker who quits or leaves the company is offered an exit interview. The company can

   - Determine the specific cause the worker chose to depart.

   - Provide details on PF, collective insurance, and the method and due date for payment.

- Find out what the staff thinks of the company's standards.

- Provide the last payment stub or details on its availability and distribution.

- Verify that the worker has delivered all textbooks, guides, equipment, and material in the exact condition.

4. **Dilemma interview**: Dilemma interviews are mostly intended for staff members who cause problems. An issue arises when a worker continues to behave or operate unacceptably despite warnings. Instead of alerts and cautions, a remedy is more probable to be suggested during an interview. A F2F conversation with the worker could help identify the cause of their poor performance. Possible causes include household issues, health issues, a lack of training, a dislike of their job, environmental issues, hierarchical issues, and more. Employees might well be provided a consultation using the counsellor sincemany organizations have counselling resources available.

5. **Stress interview**: During a stress interview, the applicants are placed under trying circumstances to see how they will handle pressure. This strategy is employed to choose candidates for jobs where the candidate has to be capable to handle challenging circumstances without becoming agitated. Applicants' bravery, tact, composure, and self-control are all tested during a stress interview because these traits are necessary whenever dealing with other people or groups.

6. **Selection interview:** Determining a candidate's eligibility for a particular position is the selection interview's primary goal.

A board of interviewers typically conducts recruitment interviews. A typical interview can last anything from 10 to 45 mins, or perhaps longer. Outstanding applicants receive an additional period during interviews. To determine whether an applicant is a good fit for the organization, they need to learn sufficiently about them.

The applicants should also learn about the company's worker regulations, culture, expectations of the hires, and prospects for professional advancement.

Examination before employment

- **Integrity exams:** One might not imagine that an exam could pinpoint employment applicants who are most inclined to cheat on their workers or engage in other unethical or illegal conduct, yet businesses have used integrity exams with a certain degree of effectiveness.

- **Personality exams** are employed to determine a person's overall moral character or appropriateness for a particular career. The particular exams determine an applicant's suitability for the psychological demands of tough jobs such as those held by aircrews, marshals, members of the cops and fire forces, and controllers of nuclear power plants (in practice, federal regulation mandates certain exams for some roles).

- **Employment skills exam**: The most popular pre-employment exam kinds evaluate a candidate's ability or particular skills required to do a position.

- **Substance exams**: Among the most divisive topics in companies nowadays is drug and alcohol screening. While certain companies see such screening as a need for maintaining professional safety, others see it as an infringement on the confidentiality of the employees and a mark of disdain. Certain businesses only evaluate job candidates and not employees.

- **Background verification:** Despite assessments in the traditional form, they do give employers extra information about oneself. While background screenings have been increasingly used 80% of U.S. businesses now do criminal background screenings, for example, drug screening might well be declining slightly.

TYPES OF INTERVIEW

Figure 24: Types of interviews

Preparation of the applicant

Not alone are the applicant's skills and understanding evaluated during the interview, but also their overall personality. The applicant needs to be ready for the interview mentally, physically, and psychologically.

1. Physical

1. The applicant is most probably to be well-groomed and appropriately attired. Standard criteria for a professional appearance include clean, well-trimmed nails, correctly coiffed hair, well-fitting clothing, tidy shoes, and a decent purse or briefcase.

2. Posture. The manner an applicant holds himself while standing, moving around, and sitting says a lot about him/her. The posture and attitude of the applicant convey their level of confidence, anxiousness, or overconfidence. Keep track of the

actions, and be sure to cease any undesirable repetitive motions.

3. Interviews require proper decorum. The applicant needs to be aware of the appropriate pleasantries for the day at a specific hour.

- Until the interviewer specifically requests a handshake, decline to do so.

- Wait until a request to sit before you do so. Get the interviewer's approval before sitting if individuals are not requested to. When moving the chair, use caution. It must not be loudly pulled. Keep a straight spine and a comfortable seat.

- If you possess a big briefcase, place it on the ground next to the chair. Keeping it on the lap is appropriate if it is smaller. Make sure you can handle your backpack with ease and practice.

- Keep your hands and elbows off the desk. When you're not employing your hands, practice maintaining them comfortably still.

- During the interview, have a relaxed posture.

- Recall saying thank you and good day to the recruiters at the start and conclusion of the interview.

2. Mental preparation

1. It is recommended for fresh employment applicants review issue topics. A current understanding of the area of specialty is required. Look over your bio and be ready to discuss your interests in additional detail.

2. At the point of the interview, questions about significant contemporary events in the nation and the globe would be

posed. We advise frequent newspaper reading, Television news listening, and conversation on contemporary events.

3. The firm's yearly statement or the online one contains facts concerning the organization where you will be having your interview, including facts about its owners and panels of directors, its products and services, its revenue, share capital, market worth, etc. The applicant should learn as much as he/she can regarding the business whose position he/she is seeking.

3. Psychological preparation

1. It's always advisable to be upfront and truthful when responding to inquiries. Typically speaking, recruiters have a negative perception of dishonesty. Being unable to respond to a query is preferable to pretending to know the reply and making an educated approximation.

2. A topical lack creates a negative impression. If there seems to be a subject that you feel uncomfortable discussing, it can be helpful to research it and practice discussing it with a handful of people.

3. The subject of compensation should be covered during the interview. It is crucial to discuss the payment deal without coming off as driven, dejected, or bargaining.

4. A applicant needs to be determined and possess a clear sense of goal to find out about their chances of being hired by the company. Before departing, facts regarding the type of responsibilities, working hours, deductions, prospective chances, additional perks, and any other requested facts should be obtained.

4. Evaluating oneself

1. A thorough self-evaluation is a requirement for accomplishment in life. Having a clear understanding of one's talents and flaws is crucial for developing self-confidence.

2. Applicants must take their opportunity and complete it properly and slowly.

3. Families as well as close friends could assist in identifying weaknesses and assisting in their correction, as well as in identifying strengths and assisting in their development.

4. A great way to prepare for an interview is to come to grips with who you are, learn ways to cope with your flaws, and utilize your strengths. It greatly boosts the personality's sense of composure and self-assurance.

Preparation of interviews

1. Interview preparations must begin far ahead. The applications that are collected are processed and examined, and suitable applicants are chosen for interviews.

2. A board of interviewers is chosen depending on the employment needs and the evaluation that must be performed during the interview.

3. A schedule for the process of the interview is set, and letters are delivered to the recruiters in addition to his chosen applicants advising them of the day, timing, and location of the interview.

4. During the interview, the interview room will take place is properly set up. Another area nearby the interview room has been set up for applicants to sit in while they are waiting to be examined.

5. A superior workplace employee and peon care to the requirements of the applicants in line. Every panel list is

required to review the bios of the applicants and develop queries depending on every applicant's bio.

6. Establish a connection to persuade the applicant to participate. If the interviewer shows respect and empathy for the applicant's requirements, the applicant would be more transparent during the conversation.

The recruiter should take into account the accompanying factors at the moment of the interview:

1. Employing the applicant's name and holding a short discussion unconnected to the interview could help to generate a comfortable mood.

2. Warm answers to the applicant's remarks help him feel at ease and prod him to proceed.

3. Regardless of whether it is clear that an applicant is inappropriate, he or she should never be made to feel degraded.

4. If a stress interview has been performed, the applicant must be informed that he/she should not be concerned regarding it following the interview.

5. Choosing a leave of absence should be fun and social, and it should be done as the applicant requests.

Guidelines of interview

The recruiter would assess your intelligence and the skills you possess acquired as a consequence of your schooling and prior expertise while keeping in mind the needs of the role. They would also look for your strengths and weaknesses aspects. Additionally, personality traits like your drive and self-presentation would be of interest to them.

Figure 25: Do's and don'ts of interviews

- Do pay attention to the recruiter's cues and suggestions, and consider if your response will be too lengthy or if the recruiter needs more details to elaborate on a statement expressed before continuing.

- Don't forget to honestly and factually describe personal abilities to the recruiter. Give particular instances of your skills that show successful results or accomplishments.

- Do be aware that the recruiter would query you regarding your abilities about the needs for the post or the selection criterion. You could anticipate being posed a query that entails using concepts to address an issue if the role demands technical or specialized understanding.

- Do ensure that you convey the idea that you are primarily focused on the tasks associated with the position than the potential for advancement or rewards the company may provide.

- Don't forget to express interest in the position you're interviewing for. Never let a chance pass you by. It is preferable to be given the option to choose another employment versus not having one, hence it is preferable to be provided the opportunity.

- Whenever you are given the chance, do ask queries.
- If you are given the chance to add something additional in your favor, do so.
- A simple "yes" or "no" response to a query is inappropriate. Provide thoughtful comments and whenever feasible, clarify yourself using instances from your expertise.
- A generic, evasive, or hesitating response is not acceptable. Never forget that only you can offer yourself to a potential employer. Create a feeling of goal and direction.
- Avoid "over-answering" inquiries. Politics or the economy might come up during the interview. It is advisable to respond to the queries truthfully and avoid rambling.
- Never criticize your current or former workers in public.
- At the preliminary interview, don't ask regarding pay, vacations, incentives, or pension. You ought to be aware of your market price, though, and be ready to describe your desired wage ranges if necessary.
- Avoid lying. Respond to queries honestly, openly, and as briefly (or "to the core") as you can.
- Don't concentrate on the bad; instead, highlight the successes and the lessons learned.

Negative interview evaluations that often result in denial encompass

- a failure to take accountability for one's conduct.
- absence of excitement and enthusiasm.
- an absence of preparedness and an inability to learn about the position and company.
- an absence of poise, bad diction, or grammar when expressing ideas.
- an absence of career guidance, aim, or objectives.

- an absence of tact, maturity, politeness, or professionalism.
- evasive - offering justifications for a subpar educational track or other negative circumstances.
- oppressive, hostile, haughty, or conceited.
- an excessive focus on cash, where people are exclusively concerned about compensation.
- a relentless "What could you do for me?" mentality.
- failing to inquire properly about the position or the company.

Ensure none of these detrimental aspects apply to you during your interview and work to conquer these obstacles so you can represent yourself more effectively during the interview.

Positivity in employment interviews

- Be prepared; perhaps the introductory short talk is a component of the interview phase.
- Make eye contact, a smile, and a name-based introduction to the interviewee.
- If the recruiter offers a hand, shake it firmly but not too tightly.
- Just grab a seat when the recruiter has extended the invitation or seated himself or herself.
- Take clues from the queries as to what they are attempting to uncover regarding you and your credentials.
- Let the recruiter take control of the dialogue.
- Avoid responding to a query before the recruiter has finished it.
- While the recruiter is speaking, pay close attention to any nonverbal cues.
- If you come across a query that could be discriminatory, think about your response before you speak.
- When the interview is ready to conclude, keep an eye out and heed for signals.

- Give the recruiter a firm handshake as well as a pleasant smile as you say goodbye and appreciate them for their time.

Unit-IV
Oral And Written Communication In Organizations
Chapter- 1
Oral Communication

Oral Communication

Figure 26: What is oral communication?

The sharing of a message or piece of facts over spoken words is known as oral communication. Both F2F communication and mechanical technologies are acceptable methods. In the organization, both would undoubtedly hold a significant role. A seminar, workshop, group discussion, individual interviews, and so on. are all examples of ways that F2F communication might take place in an organization.

The use of mechanical equipment, such as signals, telephones, mobile phones, e-mail clients, and fax machines, is crucial in today's commercial communication processes.

Oral communication seems to be a strong and extremely successful method. Accompanying some rules will help the speaker communicate effectively. The following are these guidelines:

- One should be clear about what you intend your statement to accomplish; it can be to educate, amuse, persuade, convey a viewpoint, or explain.
- Think carefully about the makeup of your audience, including their age, degree of comprehension, profession, and degree of enthusiasm for your content.
- Plan your speech in-depth. Make sure you are familiar with your primary facts and thoughts. You should also be knowledgeable about statistics.
- An excellent speaker makes the most of his voice.

Oral communication benefits

1. **Speed:** There is no significant delay between sending and receiving a message whenever you establish touch with your viewers.

2. **The communicator is capable of grabbing the listener's focus:** You may invest hours crafting a memo, note, or document just to possess the receiver scan it briefly or not comprehend it together. Nevertheless, with personal interaction, you possess far greater control over the receiver's focus.

3. **It minimizes time**: When quick action is necessary, it is preferable to communicate vocally.

4. **It minimizes expense:** One could speak with more than one individual at once, which minimizes cash when contrasted to written communication within the organization.

5. **It enables immediate comments**: When you address one or many viewers personally, you could answer queries as they come up. If you insult or mislead your listeners by using the wrong term, you could immediately change it.

6. **Complemented by non-verbal cues:** By combining oral communication with facial gestures and related non-verbal cues from the speaker's environment, the statement could be effectively comprehended by the individual hearing it.

7. **It is quite helpful** when speaking to groups during conferences, seminars, and so on.

Oral communication drawbacks

Despite its numerous benefits, oral communication may not necessarily be the optimal method. The accompanying drawbacks apply to it:

1. **Insufficient proof:** Because there is insufficient documented evidence of oral communication, its influence is simply transient.

2. Due to the limited retention capacity of humans, lengthier texts are unsuitable for this sort of communication.

3. High and time-consuming whenever the speaker and recipient are distant apart or once the persons who require to interact are isolated by a greater range, personal interaction is costly and time-consuming. Only a 1/2 hr cross-town travel could consume the majority of the afternoon or morning based on congestion or condition.

4. Hardly suitable when the subject is contentious.

5. **Extensive consideration is not feasible:** Deep thinking on the matter is not feasible since the recipient must make an instant choice in reaction to the communication obtained.

6. **Extremely susceptible to physical sound:** Oral communication is more likely to be misinterpreted due to physical noise of speaking, someone intervening in between, etc.

7. **Oral statements lack judicial** legitimacy until they are recorded and made an everlasting document.

2-way oral communication

Oral communication involves two parties: the speaker and the recipient.The various approaches to successful oral communication as a transmitter are discussed in another section part, yet as a recipient, spoken evaluations can comprise both compliments and suggestions for growth. It is beneficial to provide positive critique without disparaging the speaker's personality, just like with comments on any other project. Let's offer the accompanying advice to those who will be receiving oral or written comments on meetings:

- **Be specific.** Instead of criticizing the speaker, explain what you saw them doing. For example, instead of saying "That was a foolish manner to conclude your talk," state "I did not notice a closing sentence."

- **Be precise.** As an example, instead of saying "Your visualizations have been unsuccessful," add "I would raise the size of the font on your PPT slides since I had problems seeing the slides." This will provide the presenter with enough data to make improvements for the following session.

- Be upbeat. "Sandwich" your remarks so that you start positively, then provide constructive criticism, and finally finish positively.

- **Think positively**. Instead of just informing the presenter what they made mistakes, make concrete recommendations for growth.

- **Show compassion**. Instead of making direct comments or criticisms, use delicate wording when providing feedback. For instance, say "Communicate a little loudly so people at the end of the chamber may hear you" instead of "I couldn't catch a thing you stated up!"

- **Keep it real.** Comment on issues that the presenter could truly alter for the better. It is useless to inform a presenter they are too brief.

Guidelines for the successful presentation

A presenter must be aware of their physical language, paralanguage, presentation skills, timing, and other factors for better presentation to make oral communication.

Figure 27: How to examine the speaker and what constitutes an excellent presentation?

Listening Effectively

Understanding oral communication requires the recipient to concentrate. It is the audience's job to pay attention and put attempt to comprehend the presenter, just as the presenter possesses a role to try to be comprehended. Listening is perhaps the biggest crucial communication ability of everyone. You have a bigger obligation to hear the higher in the organization you are in.

Johnson: The capability to comprehend spoken communication and react appropriately.

M.V. Rodriques: Obtaining, interpreting, and responding to the signal obtained from the transmitter are all parts of the listening procedure.

Mr. Leland Brown: It is possible to activate and deactivate listening both intentionally and involuntarily. It begins with the recipient growing conscious of the need to pay attention and attend to what is been stated.

Process of Listening

Phase one: At this point, the audience did little more than focus on the presenter to understand the speech. You will know you have absorbed the narrator's speech if you could repeat their statements.

Phase two: This is dependent on the vocabulary, expertise, perspective, and other factors of the audience. The information is misconstrued if the audience does not appropriately perceive the terms.

Phase three: At this point, the audience chooses how to use the knowledge that has been provided.

You might decide whether to embrace what you perceive whenever you are attending a business speech. The decision you adopt at this point in the review phase is essential to the process of listening.

Phase four: The audience's reaction to the content can be expressed verbally or nonverbally. The reply informs the presenter of the audience's understanding of the content and his or her reaction.

Benefit's

1. Understanding the organization is aided by listening.

2. Listening to others can lead to improved policy decisions.

3. Listening soothes the irate workers.

4. Listening is crucial to the achievement of the open-door regulation.

5. Listening makes it easier to identify potential hazardous regions before they grow touchy.

Steps for listening effectively

1. **Eye contact:** If a listener does not fix his gaze on the presenter, he is not keen on hearing what is being said. Eye contact is a skill that a listener should display. It gives the presenter motivation.

2. **Physical displays of interest**: A listener should demonstrate that he/she is involved in what is being spoken. Nonverbal cues like suitable facial gestures, eye contact, and positive head movements could be employed to transmit meaning to the presenter.

3. **Refrain from performing any diverting motions or activities:** This includes checking one's wristwatch, shuffling documents, fiddling with pencils, reading newspapers or correspondence, and similar diverting tasks.

4. **Pose queries:** A good listener constantly checks their comprehension by asking queries to clarify any ambiguities. The presenter becomes aware that he/she is listening as a result.

5. Assist the presenter in relaxing and being conscious of the eager audience with your approach. Be experienced to listen as well as perceived to listen.

6. Resist interrupting to challenge or fight regarding things, saying things like "That is not so," "demonstrate it," and other such phrases. Following the speaker's statement, a skilled listener will comprehend what they heard.

7. **Pay careful attention:** Even if people disagree with the presenter's strategy, you still have a right to be acknowledged.

8. **No favouritism:** It is usually preferable to put aside individual opinions and attitudes regarding a presenter and his or her points of view. This is a bad habit, and the presenter occasionally feels uncomfortable as a result.

9. **Pay attention to nonverbal indications:** Look for the major ideas. Keep an eye out for nonverbal indicators that help to express meaning, such as tone of voice, body language, and others. They can be written down by the audience as they will aid in determining whether the presenter comes across as genuine in his opinions.

10. **Steer clear of acting attentive**: Numerous audiences get into the habit of acting attentive. They maintain a fixed gaze on the presenter and make an effort to come across as attentive listeners. They frequently overlook many of the speaker's crucial remarks.

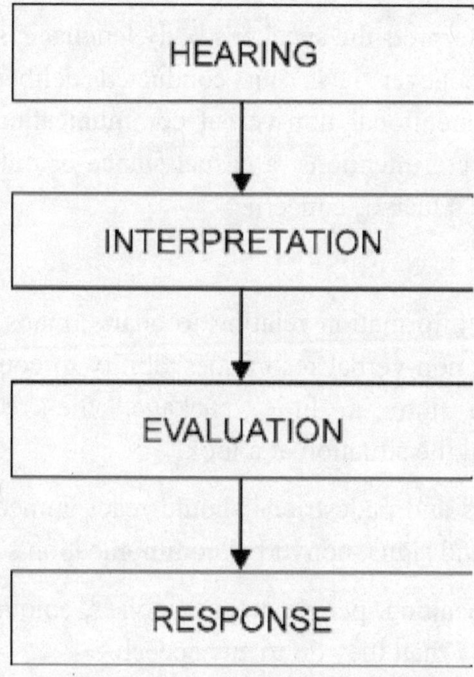

Figure 28: Process of Listening

Non-verbal communication

The term "verbal communication" describes communication that takes place via the use of phrases. Thus, verbal connection implies oral contact, and verbal proof implies oral proof. Language-free communication is referred to as non-verbal communication.

The ability to observe is directly related to nonverbal communication. The speaker must be seen to, audible to, and perhaps felt by the recipient of the communication. The person receiving the communication ought to be able to properly view the speaker's facial, posture, voice, clothes, and look, as well as hear their accent. Nonverbal communication can be both intentional and accidental because it is observed. It is intentional when the speaker makes an effort to communicate with the target audience by using deliberate gestures, stances, and various nonverbal cues. Whenever the recipient interprets the speaker's body language, stance, or look particularly whenever it is not conducted deliberately, this is considered unintentional non-verbal communication. Despite the presenter's sincere intentions, a casual stance or outfit might well be mistaken for a lack of concern.

Benefits

1. To transmit information relating to charts, maps, infographics, etc. Due to non-verbal techniques' ability to condense a lot of information into a little package, the recipient could comprehend the situation at a look.

2. Since drivers and pedestrians should react immediately to road indicators and signs, nonverbal communication seems crucial.

3. Generally speaking, people react to noises, colours, and visuals more rapidly than they do to any speech.

4. The only way to communicate with those who cannot read or write is by using nonverbal signals.

Body language

Body language refers to shifts in posture and motion that reflect a person's emotional state. Most people are not mindful of their body language, thus a large portion of it is mindless and involuntary. However, it has a significant influence on others.

There are two types of body language: unconscious and conscious

1. **Unconscious motions have a biological basis and are influenced by cultural traditions and developed habits.**

Biological: People have particular movements, attitudes, and postures due to their body types, skin tones, and facial features. Additionally, we continually work to conform our bodies to the surroundings, which might or might not be pleasant.

Habitual: In the course of adjusting oneself to the surroundings, certain gestures and gestures become learned as habits. They can also result from a job that needs continual motion or particular postures. It's also a professional tendency to use particular verb tenses and expressions.

Culture-specific practices include not crouching down in front of seniors or seniors and not staring them directly in the eyes. A few actions are also part of societal behavior, greeting practices, and introductory practices.

2. **Intentional motions, stances, and speech modulations are made. The utilization of body language is something that performers are specifically educated in, as well as strong speakers and particularly effective speakers.**

Although no one could fully regulate their body language, it is essential to increase body consciousness and have a fair degree of control over their stance, motions, and voice tone. We can better comprehend the body language of others if we become more aware of our body language.

Looks

Various factors affect a person's overall looks. Hygiene and personal grooming are 2 of the key elements that affect attractiveness. The quality of care for the face, fingernails, toes, and hair is required. A person who ignores these facets comes across negatively. First impressions are formed by looks; unkempt look, negligence in grooming, and awkward clothing leave a bad one. The looks readily reflect poor condition.

Facial gestures

The indicator of the mind, so the saying goes, is the face. The face frequently displays the emotions of the heart and the ideas of the intellect. The mindset, emotions, and response of the speakers can be expressed by the use of words or nonverbal facial gestures, such as a happy or appreciating smile, an angry frown, a surprised glance, and many other facial gestures. Some individuals have a talent for interpreting facial emotions. Effective communicators acquire to read and understand facial expressions, whether they are the presenter or the audience.

Eye contact

A crucial component of facial conduct is eye motion, which is used to attract focus, and express astonishment or enjoyment, among other emotional expressions. To show that both parties are involved in the conversation, the presenter and audience must make eye contact. When giving an oral speech, it's crucial to make eye contact using the listener to establish a connection.

Speakers consider it a goal to scan the entire group using one glance, creating fleeting eye contact with as numerous people as they can. Eye contact should only be maintained for 3 to 5 secs at most, as maintaining it longer than that can be uncomfortable for the other individual. Although it's generally accepted that minimizing eye contact shows that a presenter is dishonest, certain liars may maintain unwavering eye contact while waiting for your reaction. People who lack assurance frequently avoid making eye contact. Nevertheless, cultural norms and practices have an impact on the ways individuals utilize their eyes and faces.

Smile

One of the most effective facial expressions is a smile. It makes communication possible. A genuine, nice grin plays a significant role in forging and maintaining human connections. The proverb "You are not completely clothed until you carry a smile" beautifully highlights the importance of smiling.

Figure 29: One of the important facial expressions (smile) in oral communication

Body postures

In terms of stance, we mean how someone stands, seats, and moves. The posture of the feet, hand, and various bodily features exposes not just a person's mental condition, such as if he is lively, active, and energetic, tense and jittery, strong and self-confident, and so forth., yet additionally his/her command of the communication's topic. An effective presenter maintains a straight back, his or her feet close, his balance precisely over the instep, and his/her chin parallel to the ground or at a perfect angle to his spine. Speaking in front of an audience successfully requires that you stay in this position. A presenter who has a postural tummy and a sagging shoulder appears to be exhausted.

Your character is also displayed by the way you sit. A group discussion member will adjust his stance when it is his/her turn to talk. Nevertheless, various circumstances call for various stances. Both feet can be on the ground, one just in ahead of the other, and the back can remain straight from the hip up.

The way someone walks might reveal their level of assurance or reticence, vigour, or withdrawal.

A presenter must keep in mind that to step elegantly, they must keep their legs free at the hips, lift their feet off the ground when walking, keep their gait straight, and avoid strides or little movements.

It goes without saying that to communicate effectively, a person must learn where to put their hands while communicating, how to change their stance, and transfer their body mass from the back to the legs.

Gestures

When communicating effectively and producing useful material, gestures are crucial. The presenter's mental condition might well be revealed by gestures like fidgeting with jewellery, tightening a key chain, or firmly clasping one's hands, which can alter both the decoding and encoding of his/her content during the conversation.

A skilled communicator develops suitable gestures by practicing them in front of a mirror. Additionally, he or she asks his or her friends and co-workers for advice in this area. But when employing gestures, one must always be self-assessing, examining, and applying the proper gesture for the appropriate influence. It is likewise essential that one must exercise caution and attention when making gestures because of cultural restraints, sexual connotations, and ethical obligations. While gestures certainly add significance to communication, if they are not utilized with consideration for the period, location, and person involved, they might become uncomfortable. For instance, a greeting, a sitting posture, a thumbs-up, a hand-to-face gesture, a collar draw, thumbs and finger rubbing, eye indicators, an eye blink, and so on.

Accessories

Body language is heavily influenced by apparel. Making a subdued impact with your attire demands discretion. The dress is comprised of colour, style, cut, and fit. It is appropriate to dress in either national or modern fashion in India, giving us a variety of options. It's important to dress appropriately for the event. The formal gathering, the time of day, the seasons, the individuals who would be in attendance, their cultural backgrounds, and your own firm's traditions must all be taken into consideration. The choice of clothing accents, like ties, shoes, and jewellery, ought to be precise, and they must be at ease. Accessories consist of a purse or briefcase.

Capacity

Although it can be difficult to express enthusiasm and power as a part of body language, many individuals have felt the influence of someone who exudes a lot of power. Body language is greatly influenced by one's bodily and psychological wellness; a healthy individual is active and retains a particular degree of enthusiasm at employment. The manner of a person reflects their passion, which is frequently contagious and causes audiences to get enthused as well.

Chronemics

Individuals develop a sense of self-worth when they are allowed to hear from or chat with them. It is related to concern and caring.

On the contrary side, someone who wastes both their and other individual's time can across as ineffective and disorganized.

Proxemics

Each speaker has created or developed a particular area and territory around themselves, which they do not let others enter during communication until the presenter and recipient have a close connection. According to Edward T. Hall, there are 4 different types of range in human relationships:

1. Up to 18 inches of close physical interaction

2. Individuals, 18 inches to 4 feet.

3. Societal: four to twelve feet.

4. Audience: 12 feet for hearing and visual range

Without a doubt, each of these 4 categories has a different kind and level of communication activity. Yet keep in mind that we each choose these places for ourselves and that we could alter them by moving. They are therefore unique to us as individuals. Space separation varies from culture to culture. The communication process and the contents of the signal can occasionally be harmed by space distance. The usual distance, meanwhile, can be disregarded in a psychological state that is emotionally intense.

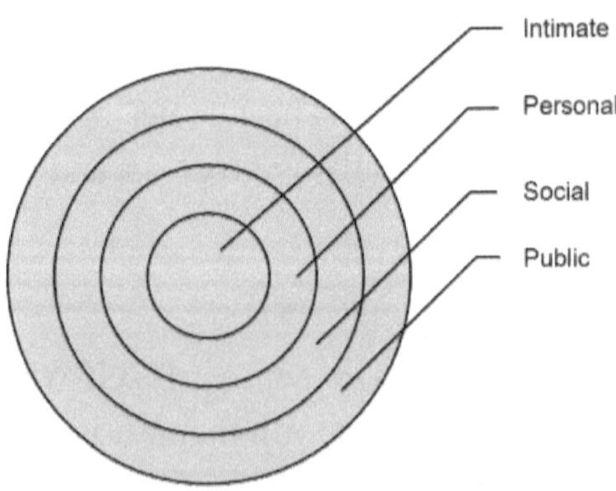

Figure 30: Proxemics

Language

Paragraph language refers to the uttered words' nonverbal components. It encompasses the characteristics of the voice, how we utilize it, and the utterances we emit without saying them. By becoming conscious of it and paying regard to one's tone and words, one can successfully regulate and utilize paragraph language.

Voice possesses traits like

- The tone of a voice refers to its texture.
- Volume can indeed be intentionally changed depending on the crowd size, as well as the distance separating the presenter and the audience. Communicating too loudly demonstrates incompetence or an aggressive personality.
- The low or high chord on the range is known as pitch. In addition to being uncomfortable and denoting immaturity or emotional instability, an individual who is afraid will frequently communicate in a high-pitched tone. It is preferable to start quietly and with a low tone before increasing the volume as needed.

Speech has a speed component. Speaking quickly conveys eagerness. We speak more quickly when telling an engaging tale and less quickly when attempting to convey a challenging concept.

The established norm for how to pronounce a word is called pronunciation. It is accurate and clear is crucial since it shows that a communicator is attentive to details and takes the listeners' interests into account.

The pronunciation of a language is referred to as an accent. We apply the accent from our native language to other languages since each language possesses its unique manner of producing sounds. Relating to natural communicators of a language will help you develop a pleasant dialect.

In a statement, adding emphasis to a specific word can alter its inference and meaning. What you accomplished at the last conference? can be read by underlining various words, and you can compare the implied meanings of the various words. Occasionally, when a communicator is unsure how to pronounce a word, they will emphasize it by using words like Mmmmm, Ouch, Huh, and so on.

Being silent may be a highly powerful form of communication. It involves a lot of self and self-assurance to be capable to restrain one's tongue, making silence a tough form of communication to adopt. The emphasis that can be added to words with brief gaps or silences is particularly effective. Particular phrases stick out from the others when there is a pause before or after them. The audience can become more attentive with a well-timed pause. However, some of it serves as a hindrance to communication, like when speaking on the cell phone when one party cannot view the other's reaction on their face.

Chapter- 2

Written Communication

Planning and Organizing of Business Writing

The greatest approach to guarantee that a writing activity will indeed be effective is to break it down into the next 5 phases:

- Preparing,
- Organizing,
- Investigation,
- Draft Writing, and
- Revision

These 5 phases should initially be performed actively, particularly deliberately to oneself. The phases in all of these procedures eventually get almost automated.

They offer 3 key suggestions under "preparation." Establishing the document's objective is the first step. In other terms, you ought to choose what you want your viewers to take away from the paper. Then, we come back to this. The second step is to "evaluate your reader" to determine what degree of term or jargon will indeed be appropriate and what the viewer previously knows.

Establishing the "context of the writing task" is the last step. To put it another way, how much information must you gather or incorporate to ensure that your paper serves its intended aim?

The most effective order in which to communicate your concepts is what these writers refer to as organizing.

Whenever we discuss information organizing subsequently, we address this. They explore employing the "style of growth" that is "most suitable," a topic we will also cover subsequently in this section.

This method is advocated in several texts on corporate communication, which claim that composing is effectively accomplished by following a predetermined order of operations. The phases are labelled differently by numerous authors, yet the concepts are extremely comparable. Depending on writings that emphasize word processing or printed materials, this figure was created. We might also consider if this phased technique can be used for Web sites since numerous organizations now post a variety of materials online.

Heller and Hindle (1998)	Stanton (1996)	Barker (1999)
Decide what you want to say	Write down your purpose	Create a message
Research the information	Assemble the information	
	Group the information	
	Put the information into logical sequence	Organize the information
Write your draft	Produce a skeleton outline	
	Write the first draft	Write a first draft
Edit and revise	Edit and write the final draft	Edit and revise

Figure 31: Principles to follow while writing for business, according to several experts

Years of study into human observation, intelligence, and memory have shown us that the human brain constantly predicts, organizes, and reorganizes the facts it obtains. Most of the time, we are unaware of the volume or scope of these processes. As a consequence, how information is presented has the potential to deceive us. In his overview of studies on human problem-solving and decision-making, Scott Plous makes a very strong case for this. For instance, he cites studies that invited learners to remark on video footage of automobile fatalities.

When prompted to evaluate the rate of the vehicles when they "hammered," respondents indicated an average rate that was 30% greater than whenever prompted to evaluate the rate of the vehicles when they "struck." When questioned about "smashed" vehicles, participants were also more prone to "remember" a week afterward that the collision contained shattered glass, which has been not depicted in the film snippets. In other terms, these participants had not merely recalled the mishap; instead, they had built a picture of it around the idea of a "smash," and unconsciously inflated some of the details they had witnessed. Other studies have demonstrated the effectiveness of recommendations in specific query forms; for instance, asking "how extensive was the video" as opposed to "how brief was the motion picture" affects a person's estimations. Therefore, how information is conveyed affects our ability to remember and comprehend it. Without a precise format, content is difficult for us to recall or assimilate.

This demonstrates the idea that, even while categorization aids in the organization of the facts, we must adopt a method of categorization that is reliable and employs just one criterion at a moment. Of course, sub-categorization is a possibility. One might also require to select parameters that suited the topic and the viewer's demands if one has been attempting to aid individuals in remembering a table of this kind. For instance, a food categorization might be more intriguing to an animal nutritionist than a zoological categorization.

Researchers have made an effort to demonstrate the requirement for the planned organization in even the most straightforward written communication. This can range from a 3-4 points framework for an answer to a note of inquiry to a framework with subheadings and headings for an exploratory study, and we'll provide instances of both in the following parts. Today's word processing programs come with an outliner, allowing one to enter their content either on a regular sheet or immediately into the outliner. One can examine the work in outline at a particular moment, supplied the employed the level of headings that the word processor permits. It may be simpler to use "cut

& paste" in regular mode while moving content about in outline mode.

Therefore, one could create an outline directly in the document processors to check if their concept seems reasonable before expanding it. One young admin, for instance, was required to write a brief presentation on restoring the carpeting inside the head office. He began by outlining the accompanying:

- accessible carpet characteristics and suitability for diverse work environments;
- the price of the different levels;
- colour options (requires brochure illustrating colour schemes);
- fitting services provided by regional businesses;
- assurances.

One could employ the outliner tool to create an action plan as a guideline before you begin your inquiry for larger papers, like reporting on studies. This could be elaborated upon once the inquiry is finished in the study's outline. For instance, if individuals were requested to research your company's copier requirements for the following 5 years, your strategy may resemble this:

- existing copying capabilities;
- projections of upcoming needs;
- contemporary and emerging technologies;
- running expenses;
- backup plan and spare parts.

One might expand this idea into a further detailed blueprint when the data has been gathered and examined. For instance, while looking at operational expenses, you should compare the expenses of buying versus leasing as well as the various types of leasing that are offered.

Substantial improvements in the manner computer software assist our writing via features like outliners and other advancements are anticipated to happen in the coming seasons.

Hybridizing structures with objectives

The organization of the written communication must complement your goals, which is the foremost crucial factor (this is also applicable to F2F communication). We may demonstrate this by considering potential formats for a persuasive letter. Several of the components that might be present comprise the ones below. The following components are listed in no particular order and are not always necessary:

- A captivating opening,
- a declaration of the circumstance,
- a description of the recipient's requirements or benefits,
- a description of the sender's requirements,
- a visualization of the conclusion,
- a balancing of the requirements of the sender and the recipient, and
- an active call is all necessary.

Where can go wrong in business writing?

Business communication primarily consists of 2 attributes: how the company interacts with its clients and the general audience, and how the company communicates with one another. Both of these facets of professional writing have received plenty of critiques. Wind & Main (1998) state in their analysis of exterior communication that "enterprise performs an extremely lousy work of expressing oneself, and too frequently gets its feet in its mouth." They keep criticizing how business people behave, saying that "on TV, CEOs come across as mouth-tied grouches, as well as business talk, suffocates discourse."

They use the accompanying statement from an inventive American corporation as an illustration of the "motionless" and jargon-filled language that they perceive as characteristic of business talk: HR goes beyond the conventional personnel role by working with inner consumers to identify effective answers to individual-based problems and needs. What could this signify to somebody who is not highly knowledgeable in conceptual discussions around personnel practice? likely not much at all! Regrettably, the organization might suffer from this linguistic usage. It could convey an impression of pretentious or exaggerated communication, which breeds suspicion, instead of attracting an outside audience.

What could we accomplish when business writing seems so frequently unclear, excessively complicated, and ugly? We ought to take William Horton at his word when he says that we require a new class of business document—"one that replies to problems in a rush." Adopting Plain English has indeed been a quite typical reaction. Before delving deeper into this, it is important to look at the broad standards that are frequently used in business writing to choose a proper style.

Improved letter	Comment
REMOVAL OF OFFICE CONTENTS	
Thank you for your letter of 30 June about moving the contents of your offices. We wish to confirm the following points from our telephone conversation.	Gives an immediate audience orientation.
We are able to move the contents of your offices at 08:00 on 20 July as required. We have provisionally included your move in our work schedule.	Immediately confirms that the work can be done.
Mr S Strydom will visit you at 09:00 on 6 July to prepare a quotation and he will submit this to you within 24 hours.	There is no unnecessary information here.
We will hold your move on our removal schedule until 12 July to give you time to decide on our quotation. If there is anything you wish to know about these arrangements, please contact me at 706 2345(ext. 6781).	Gives a definite date. Also clarifies how the customer can respond.
Yours sincerely	
W Smith Removals Manager	

Figure 32: How to make a business letter better?

What does business writing's "excellent style" mean?

"Option in the style of writing is important". Although if your workplace has very clear guidelines for how messages and files should be written, you would nevertheless need to adopt decisions about what language to employ, how to structure the paragraphs, and other issues. To design a document with the proper contents and style, you would need to make creative decisions. We'll look into these 2 factors to find the "optimal" business approach.

Criteria of contents

What standards may we apply to assess a business text's content? Even though numerous works on corporate communication concentrate on the initial 3, the following constitute the most typical:

1. Accuracy

The most crucial factor in business writing involves accuracy. Content that is improper and erroneous can frequently be very destructive than data at all. Would you want to fly on a plane that had been maintained using an incorrect guide?

However, this poses the question of how precise the writing should be. It frequently takes a lot of details and qualifying of the facts to achieve a significant level of accuracy. The end effect can be overly wordy documents that nobody wants to comprehend.

2. Brevity

The aforementioned instance does not meet the requirement for brevity. Overly wordy writing and/or unneeded information are the typical causes of lengthy texts. The writer should ascertain what the viewer understands, what the viewer requires to understand, and what the reader desires to understand because they typically have additional facts than they do.

Once they are certain of this, one could edit the statement without omitting crucial details. If we take the memo above into consideration, we can pose the corresponding queries:

- Is knowing the poll's actual date necessary or desired?
- Are the researchers' titles important?
- What degree of precision is required?

The wording of the memorandum can indeed be condensed to the accompanying when we keep in mind that the document (whereby the supervisor could examine to verify it) has all of the specific details:

Regarding your inquiry about perceptions of a canteen.

We conducted a questionnaire-based study of staff opinions. 70 percent of the employees were polled, and 90 percent of them agreed. Here is a copy of our study.

This cuts the paragraph in half, from 136 to 34 words, or 75%. Yes, there is such a thing as too much brevity. An employee canteen is preferred by 90 percent of the employees, which could be summed up in just 7 terms. However, the viewer would have a harder time remembering the context of the demand if they read this statement. The accuracy issue is another issue; in reality, 90% of 70% had been in support. In light of this, clarity is the following standard.

3. Clarity

Insufficient clarity is frequently the result of bad writing instead of complex subject matter, and it can be brought on by things like stilted language and cliches, extensive recurrence and description, an absence of a structured way, and overuse of abstract and general vocabulary.

4. Emphasize

You must emphasize essential facts. How can we choose what is significant, though? It is data that will assist your writer's ideas and facts that are significant to the readers.

- Less crucial content must be omitted or put subsequently in the script.
- These standards allow for additional improvement of the prior article.

There are additional ways to emphasize things besides ranking them in terms of significance, like the ones listed below:

Format and typeface. It is possible to draw attention to crucial details in a report by using its design and typography. White room, checklists, bulleted points, and headlines are a few examples of approaches.

Grammatical construction. Creating a term for the statement's topic allows us to draw attention to it. For instance, you may state "An optic pyrometer detected the temperature" as opposed to "The temperature has been determined by an optical pyrometer." This emphasizes the importance of the assessment methods.

Of all, emphasis shouldn't be used to the extent that it distorts the truth or obscures crucial facts.

Written communication

Whenever oral communication is not an option, written communication is the most appropriate form of communication. Managers in all firms can effectively communicate between and within departments by sending written comments. The act of communicating entails conveying written messages. All types of subject content are covered in written communication, including bulletins, memos, studies, financial reports, business correspondence, and so on. The method of condensing a statement into writing that is widely utilized in organizations is merely referred to as this form of communication. Formal communications, like regulations, instructions, guides, policy issues, etc., should constantly be in writing.

Written Communication

Merits

- Accurate
- Precise
- Permanent record
- Legal document
- Can reach a large number of people simultaneously
- Helps to fix responsibility.

Figure 33: Advantages of written communication

Goal of writing

One of the crucial components of communication is the orderly storage of written correspondence.

Since humans have weak memory, filing and indexing are both important. Written communication should be preserved so that it can be quickly and efficiently provided when required. The primary reason for composing the messages is revealed, nevertheless, in the succeeding.

1. Prospective references: It is impossible to ignore the limitations of the human mind and its weak memory capacity. Written communication can be kept as a document or a resource of information. Different forms of communication could indeed be archived for later use. Consequently, maintaining documents is necessary for the ongoing functioning of the firm.

2. Preventing Errors: Prior files assist in decreasing errors and omissions during data transmission, as well as in preventing fraud.

3. Requirements of the law: Written correspondence is admissible as official documentation. For this reason, some business

leaders believe that even when statements are delivered verbally, they must afterward be validated in writing.

4. Broad access: As a result of the rapid development of communication technologies, written communication is now widely available. Written communication conveyed via postal mail or email is the least expensive and could be the primary possible method of communication connecting the speaker and the recipient if they are far apart.

5. Making good decisions: Having access to old records is quite helpful. When historical files are accessible, decision-making is simplified.

Principle of efficient writing

1. Unity: The idea of unity in composition suggests the necessity of unity. On three different stages, the unity concept is valid. The various lines should initially be combined. Secondly, each paragraph needs to flow smoothly. Thirdly, the statement should be cohesive as a whole.

2. Coherence: The notion of coherence ought to be present in a written message to establish clarity. Relationship and simplicity are two crucial components of coherence. The statement in general and each line, paragraph, and clause must all be coherent.

3. Steer clear of jargon: The writer must steer clear of jargon whenever feasible. Jargon is indeed a language that is specific to a given field of study, industry, trade, or career. The jargon might be used in conversation with experts in the area in confidence. Jargon may be employed in other circumstances, yet hardly if it is evident to everyone else.

4. Accuracy: The information presented should be true and accurate. The content should be conveyed in the right way.

Proper reviewing and editing could help writers be more accurate.

5. Brevity: Writing must be more concise by employing fewer words to convey more ideas. Being concise not just preserves effort yet also makes writing more elegant. Business communications should be succinct and direct.

6. 7 Cs of communication: Kindly refer to unit 1.

Word choice and adaptation

Efficient writing strategies include an emphasis on simplicity when employing words, brief lines, and compact paragraphs, as well as simplicity regarding adaption. Words are changed to fit the statement and the viewer in question. The capability to interpret a statement, one's vocabulary, and one's level of subject expertise are not universal among readers. Therefore, in to communicate effectively, we need to be aware of the other party. The statement ought to make sense to the recipient. For these grounds, it is recommended to use the accompanying approaches when writing.

• Use well-known terms

Regrettably, a lot of business writers frequently alter their tone when they start to write because they don't utilize sufficient everyday language.

• Opt for the shorter term over the longer one.

Big words tend to distract the viewer, therefore shorter terms typically communicate effectively.

Several big terms are so widely recognized that communication is simple, including hypnosis, hippopotamus, and vehicle. And just a select handful of people can understand certain short terms like vibrations, vie (to finish), vex (angry or disturbed), and scab (employee).

Therefore, it would be good for one to utilize big terms sparingly. Additionally, you must make certain that your viewer will be comfortable with those you do utilize.

• Be careful while using technical terms.

Technological terms, or "jargon," are used in all areas and constitute a portion of our daily functioning language. In addition, it would seem so frequent in your head that you would think that individuals outside of the areas are also aware of it. And you might utilize these phrases when writing to people who are not in your industry, which causes misunderstandings.

Building a logical paragraph

Writing requires more than just selecting terms carefully and creating concise phrases. It also refers to the properly constructed paragraph. Similar to how syllables are paired to form sentences, sentences are also arranged logically in paragraphs.

The progression from 1 line to the next and the gradual development of the paragraph represent one's mental procedure. It takes skill to organize and connect facts in a planned paragraph. It calls for the application of reason and creativity.

Qualities of a strong paragraph:

1. **Cohesion:** A paragraph ought to possess cohesion, much like lines. One notion or concept must be covered in each paragraph. The conclusion of the paragraph needs to convey a sensation of completeness.

2. Coherence: A excellent paragraph flows smoothly from 1 line to the next. Each line needs to make sense about the one before it and the one after it. The flow of ideas between sentences should be evident.

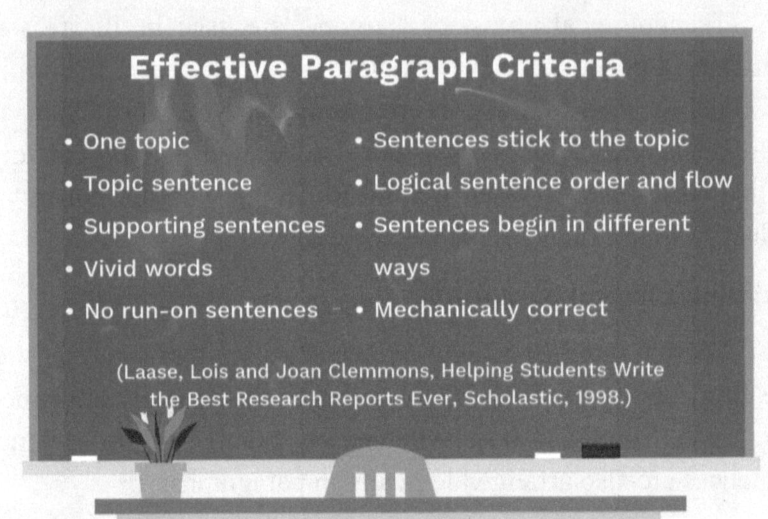

Figure 34: Qualities of a strong paragraph

3. Length: The paragraph's length ought to be just right neither too lengthy nor too small. The length of a paragraph will depend on what it contains. For messaging, smaller paragraphs are acceptable.

A concise paragraph makes it easier for the viewer to comprehend the paper's organization. Furthermore, shorter paragraphs are easier on the eyes. Individuals merely prefer reading items that offer them breaks frequently. The gap shouldn't happen too often though. A string of brief paragraphs creates an unattractive jagged impression.

4. Using subject lines to convey a paragraph's core concept is the strongest effective approach to organizing a paragraph, according to research. The subsequent phrases then reinforce and elaborate on it. The subject lines function as the paragraph's title in a way, and the rest of the phrases provide the rest of the tale.

Topic lines are not necessary for each phrase, though. According to the author's plan, the theme phrases could appear initially, finally, or in the mid.

5. Excessive detail omission: Just the facts that are required should be introduced. You require judgment to determine what you require. Place oneself in the author's shoes to make the most accurate judgment.

1. How will it be utilized?

2. What will be utilized?

3. What won't be utilized?

After that, decide. Following this process will possibly result in omitting a lot of what you had planned to utilize.

General Tone

1. Style of conversation

Write in a conversational tone with effective language. The language you employ must be drawn from the spoken vocabulary, and the writing style should encourage casual discussion.

That writing seems to generate compassion in all of us. It brings to mind good interactions with amiable folks. Furthermore, it is the most effective form of language for communication as it employs terms that are recognizable to speakers of our language.

Each moment a specific circumstance arises, people automatically utilize terms known as rubber stamps. We utilize them without giving them any thought. They administer standard care instead of individualized care. Furthermore, normal care plays a much less role in building positive public relationships than special focus. While writing in their everyday language, you could prevent rubber stamps.

2. You-view method

The human species is a selfish one. Statements that speak to your self-interest, therefore, elicit a beneficial reaction. You-view point is the name of this method.

Writing from your perspective highlights your audience's passions. It is a mindset that puts the viewer's perspective front and core.

3. Courtesy

Goodwill in correspondence is greatly influenced by courtesy. Of course, communicating in a conversational style, deliberately highlighting the viewer's perspective, and properly using pleasant wording would lead to civility. All would contribute significantly to the viewer's positive mental state. Refrain from preaching (giving a lecture) and staying angry.

4. Sincerity

Sincere attempts should go into being polite. Engaging in the writing letter strategies you employ leads to sincerity. Your writing would demonstrate your genuineness. 2 key criteria for creating authentic letters are:

(a) Excessive goodwill: There is such a thing as excessive goodwill. Too many you-view points come off as fake.

(b) Steer clear of exaggeration: Exaggeration is an overreaction of the truth. While some exaggeration is common in sales writing, there are still acceptable limits. We seldom actually embrace phrases like "amazing," "amazing," "sensational," "revolution," "perfection," and so forth.

Process of e-writing

Writing takes on exciting novel forms as a result of the additional requirements that e-communication places on language. Electronic media, recognized as a potent teaching tool, has not just transformed the writing procedure yet has likewise been discovered to promote engagement in writing activities. E-mail and web conversations offer a non-threatening environment in that authors seem less constrained regarding revealing themselves, which encourages particularly shy individuals who typically decline to talk in F2F conversations to openly engage in online conversations.This is one explanation for this. Another explanation is that the Internet gives authors a platform to share their work with a genuine, extensive population that goes outside the confines of the class and institution. Learners are inspired to write whenever they recognize that their effort will be published online by people who live in the actual world.

Collaboration writing practices have been proven to grow with the use of the internet. Concerning whether it exerts an equivalent impact on the volume and grade of writing produced by particular pupils, there are differing opinions. The e-medium enhances learners' perspectives regarding writing and practicing the targeted language and motivates them to generate additional text since it lessens the fear component and provides appealing characteristics.

- Pre-writing: Studying a subject and coming up with a theme are two pre-writing exercises. Multimedia actions that might indeed occur during this phase of the writing procedure include idea creation through team brainstorming, questioning through e-mail, engaging in big groups, noticing graphical depictions on the Web, perusing collected data digitally, discovering CD ROMs, and connecting e-libraries.

Figure 35: Electronic writing process

- Creating and noting are two types of writing activities. A multimedia setting could aid the approach at this point. Multimedia possibilities for this phase of the procedure include scheduling and highlighting an article with the specialized application, creating a rough draught with speech-recognizing apps, inspecting images and text, and inserting statistics straight on the display rather than writing by hand and afterward translating to the display.

- Rewriting: Tasks involving rewriting include editing and fixing. This phase of the procedures can be impacted by multimedia by enabling voice recognition to replace keyboarding for add, cut, and paste patterns, utilizing a spell checker, listening to essays or articles employing writing system identification apps, and employing interactive voice-activated apps to rectify orthography, syntax, and grammar.

- Post-writing: Multimedia provides enabled post-writing tasks, which are a natural extension of the writing procedure. This stage of the writing procedure is given novel significance by editing and distribution via e-tools. Essays are no longer required to be linear and in 2 dimensions as they once were. The manner that information or research findings are conveyed and exhibited in a classroom context can be altered by the addition of hue, animation, graphics, voice, & video to a textual. Presently, in complement to the conventional textual display, learners are displaying the outcomes of their research in various ways. To fully assess students' work, instructors will require to possess accessibility to a multimedia setting. The choice of the ultimate collection of actions would take into account, particularly the preferred way of distribution. Student activities would inspire and entice more people than an assignment if it is distributed online. Multimedia classroom assignments would be subject to ongoing revision and restructuring of learners' cognitive output, providing a realistic representation of the writing procedure in the actual world.

- This multimedia-oriented paradigm suggests that writing is deeper than just a series of activities, which has implications for the writing approach. When writing, a variety of abilities and dispositions can come along for a certain goal. Each of the 4 phases outlined here can include cycles and branches using multimedia. We suggest that writing be viewed as a collection of interactive and iterative procedures that come along not only for the creation of written content yet also for the true multimedia display of cognitive stimulation in a constantly expanding context.

Unit-V

Business Letters and Reports Formulation

Chapter-1

Business Letters

Objective

- Reviewing the fundamentals of writing business letters
- To improve the way business statements are written.
- This will involve updating the following:

To stay in touch with the outside environment, which includes other businesspeople, clients, and governmental agencies, we require to create business letters. Additionally, for corporate uses such as workplace instructions, circulars, memos, and so on. For a local firm, producing a letter might not be as crucial, yet it still has value.

There are other forms of communication as well, such as the telephone and telegraph, yet they could just leave a brief effect on the recipient. These media decrease the likelihood that the content will be retained in mind over the period.

The primary method of communicating is through sending business letters. Business letters continue to be significant in corporate communication amid the widespread use of email for inner and exterior communication. A business letter includes all of the benefits of written communication such as that it may be preserved and referenced at any time and is a binding regulatory record.

The format of a business letter differs from that of a personal letter. This chapter suggests reviewing business letter composing fundamentals with learners because a business letter symbolizes the company.

Business letter function

- The business letter is a document that can be referred to in the future. Back references are common in corporate communication. Just whenever past activities, contracts, and so on involving users, providers, and the kind are maintained in writing could they be accessed conveniently, promptly, and accurately?

- It is employed to broaden the region of activities because it may approach any place and makes a long-lasting imprint on the recipient's consciousness than oral communication.

- It functions as a regulatory record.

- It is employed to generate goodwill.

Different letter types

Personal writings are casual and are used to convey information or seek acceptance; writing to friends and family are examples of personal letters. Personal writings are composed in a pleasant, casual tone. When nonpersonal letters are employed for commercial purposes, they must be composed formally. The specific form is determined by the firm. There are several types of non-personal or business letters:

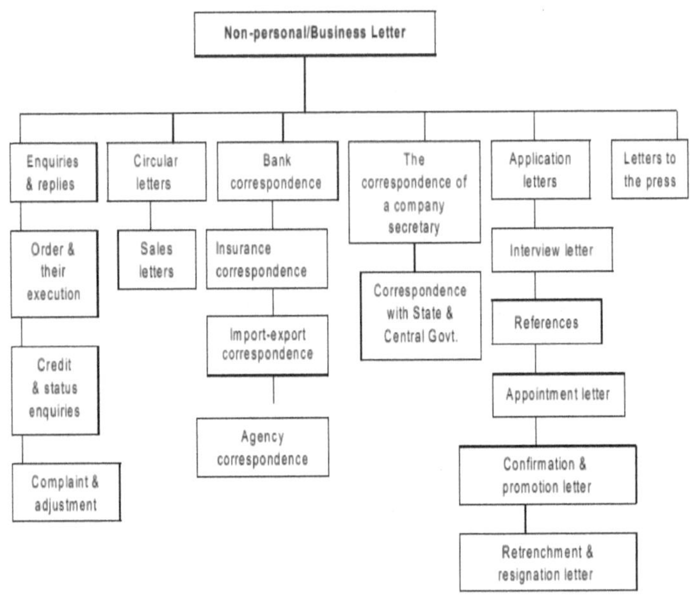

Figure 36: Different kinds of business letters

On a large scale, the accompanying is commonly utilized in organizations:

1. Official letters are typically sent to official or semi-government organizations.

2. Demi-official notes (D.O.) have an official function yet are issued to a specific individual by title. If a situation needs the addresses to personally handle it, if it is private, or if it is important and needs to be resolved right away, a D.O. letter might well be prepared.

3. Both administration and corporate organizations employ inner memos or letters for inner communication.

4. Form letters are employed for correspondence that is frequent or repetitive character. They serve as a reference for the pertinent

information included in this letter, such as acknowledgments, notifications, interviews, notices, and appointments.

Elements of business letters

1.   **Heading:** For communication with external parties, the majority of business firms employ their printable letters. The name, location, mobile number, and, if applicable, the telegraph contact information are all listed on the letterhead. The address and name are typically placed at the upper central core of the sheet, with any other details being specified in the margins.

2. **Date:** Certain letterheads have a printed line that indicates where the date must be entered, while others allow the writer to decide where to put it. It needs to be entered 2 places after the letterhead's final line. On the top right side, the date, month, and year ought to be written as

2nd August, 2001

2 August, 2001

August 2, 2001

   (Of the 3, only the last two choices are accurate.)

3. **Reference:** 2 sentences are sometimes included on letterheads to list citations:Offer the citation number over the 2nd sentence and the correspondent's citation number over the initial if you are responding.Some businesses chose to include the correspondent's citation number in the letter's body.

4. **Internal address**: When there is no focus sequence or section above the greeting, the entire address of the individual or firm you are mentioning must be communicated 2 spaces above the greeting and 2 spaces underneath the date. The names of people, businesses, street corners, roads, etc., must be communicated exactly as they are in the source from which

you obtained the address. These specifics shouldn't be compressed. Doing so is improper corporate conduct. It is also important to pronounce the address name accurately. If you pronounce his/her name wrong, he/she might think you do not care about him/her. There are different dispatch sections in numerous businesses. What you type as the inner address in this part will be replicated on the card. Your letter might not get to its intended recipient if you failed to correctly include the inner address.

5. **Attention line:** A letter that is sent to a corporate or company may occasionally be designated to a specific official in that organization to guarantee rapid attention. An attention line should be added to 2 spaces underneath the inner address & 2 spaces over the greeting to accomplish this.

6. **Salutation:** It is, a crucial component of a letter, similar to how you embrace someone when you first meet them. It is positioned 2 spaces underneath the attention line, or 2 spaces underneath the inner address if there isn't one.

The interior address's company and the composer's and viewer's interpersonal connection influence the salutation option. Employ "Dear Sirs" when writing to a business, corporation, panel, society, club, or government body. Constantly keep in mind that the salutation is unaffected by the attention line. Dear Sir or Dear Smt would be used as the salutation if you are writing a letter to an official by name.

7. **Subject:** The goal of the subject section is to make it clear to the viewer what the letter is concerning. It reduces effort in the same way that focuses and referencing sections do. The convention is to compose this sentence with a double space separating it and the greeting and the initial sentence of the letter's body.Nevertheless, other businesses choose to place the subject section before the greeting and after the attention line.

8. **Body:** The primary goal of a letter seems to be to communicate content, and the primary goal of the statement is to elicit the desired reaction from the audience. Mostly via the letter's body, this is accomplished. As a result, it is crucial to arrange and display the information appropriately.Reference to any prior communication must be made in the initial paragraph, and the primary point must be presented in the next.One should make it obvious in the concluding paragraph whatever activity you are counting on the viewer to perform. Alternatively, you can close the letter by outlining your hopes, desires, or goals. Until the letter seems quite lengthy and covers several significant topics, no headers are used for the paragraphs.

9. **A complimenting conclusion** is a polite approach to taking a break from absence when concluding a letter. It is written 2 spaces underneath the final sentence of the letter's body. The salutation needs to be in harmony with the complimenting conclusion.

10. **Signed name:** The author's name appears as the signature. The complementing closure is positioned over it. A signature can be printed with room to spare 4 spaces underneath the concluding sentence, where the writer's name is often placed.

11. **Typist recognition markings**: Located 1 or 2 spaces underneath the signature, these markings are placed on the left side of the margin of the letter to indicate the letter's writer. The investigator's initials are often placed foremost on letters that are addressed to him.

For instance, if Km. Parul Gupta composed the letter after Sri S.P. Shukla had narrated it.

Vashudha Radio Corporation
Lajpat Nagar, New Delhi

25th August 2007
Messrs. M.P. Khera & Bros.(P) Ltd.
25, Lodhi Road
New Delhi

Confidential

Dear Sirs,

The firm named below wishes to open an account with us for Rs.50,000, 3 months and has given your name as a credit reference.

Any information you may furnish us will be treated as strictly confidential.

We shall appreciate an early reply and assure you of our willingness to reciprocate at any time. A stamped, addresses envelope is enclosed for your convenience.

Yours faithfully
Ms. M. Suman
Credit Manager

Figure 37: Example of inquiry and status business letter

12. **Attachments:** If the letter has any attachments, they should be listed against the enclosing section, which is entered 2 spaces underneath the recognition markings. The standard format is to enter the shortened form Encl., alongside which the count of enclosing is given.

13. **Replica distributions**: In certain cases, replicas of a letter must be delivered to recipients in addition to the addressee. In these situations, the identities of these individuals must be put immediately beneath the referencing initials or the enclosing indication, if applicable. The identities of the individuals must be listed either chronologically or in ascending order of significance.

14. **Postscript**: A postscript is indeed a sentence that is added following the letter is finished. A postscript (P.S.) is a sign that the composer did not adequately organize his correspondence or that he/she neglected to mention whatever is crucial in the letter's body. It must ideally be eliminated from the perspective of a successful business P.S.

Range of layout

1. Stationery: White sheets are used since they help the lettering shine out more plainly and facilitate comprehension.Business letters are often written on paper that is 18 1/2 by 11 inches in size. Additional sizes include 8 x 10, 5 x 10, and 5 and a half x 8 and a half inches.

2. Typing: Many business correspondences are typed. There are 2 factors at play. The saving effort by typing also provides the letter with a neat aesthetic. Nevertheless, attention must be paid to how cleanly the characters are typed.

3. Margins: Margins enhance the appeal of a letter. In a regular-size letter, there should typically be a 1-inch margin on each side on the bottom and top.

4. Envelope: The envelope size must match the sheet on which the text is composed. When using a screen envelope, the letter must be folded so that the inner address is visible. The bare minimum number of bends ought to be utilized.

Arrangement of a business letter's parts and layouts

Layout describes the methodical grouping of a business letter's elements for improved comprehension. Business letters can be formatted in a variety of ways, including Block, Altered, Semi-Block, Suspended Indention, and Demi-Official. Studying the letter's more popular formats will be sufficient. which are

- For business letters, this complete block format is frequently employed. All the elements are placed closer to the left side of the margin in this arrangement. The paragraphs are spaced using a 2-line format. The sender's and recipient's credentials are written using accessible punctuation, which indicates that commas are omitted from this part of the sentence. Additionally, there are zero commas following the complementing closing. This makes the letter look tidy and uncomplicated. With all the parts pushed to the left side of the margin, it is an easy form to type on. Nevertheless, certain individuals consider it unbalanced because of this.

- Modified Block: It is a layout that is used frequently in contemporary Indian business writing. To break up the monotonous of the Complete Block Format, it changes it. The dates and the complements are moved to the right-hand side of the margin, moving 2 of the elements. Other characteristics resemble those of the whole block form.

- Semi-Block: This is how letters are often written. To make the letter seem fair, the area is separated equally. At the front core of the sheet, the user's contact is placed, followed by the date, the inner address, the greeting, and the complement information. The sections start 5 spaces after the left side of the margin, whereas the subject sentence is placed closer to the margin.

- Using a hanging indention format is similar to using a block design, with the exception that all subsequent sentences in every paragraph should be separated by 4 or 5 spaces. Its distinctive look might draw notice fast, yet this feature could also work against it. By drawing the viewer's interest to the letter's appearance instead of its content, it can divert him. In the business sector, this fashion was not well-liked.

- The biggest current attempt in layout design is the NOMA shape. The National Office Managing Association of America endorses it (NOMA). Additionally recognized there is in the UK. The majority of the attributes of the complete block format are present. The left side of the margin as well as the block style's inner address is where each line starts. This form's unique characteristics are:

(i) There is neither an answer nor a complementing conclusion.

(ii) Three lines underneath the inner address, in uppercase letters, is the subject line;

(iii) Listing elements with numbers start at the left side of the margin; otherwise, the elements are indented five spaces. Entries do not terminate with a full stop.

(iv) Underneath the place for a sign, the narrator's identity and position are placed in all capital letters.

(v) The composer's initials have been located in the bottom left corner.

Name & Address of the Company

Date ....

Inside Name & Address ....

....

Subject ....

....

....

....

.... Body of Letter ....

....

....

....

Signature & Designation

Figure 38: Example of NOMA format

Cs of business letter composing: guidelines

The most common type of business correspondence is business letters, which can be written physically (physical or hard copy) or electronically (soft copy). Business letters are prepared for a variety of purposes, including asking and responding to questions, managing complaints, managing consumer connections, marketing items, asking for credits, gathering payments, and gaining the client's goodwill. The letter should guarantee that the required activity is taken and that the intended response is received. As a result, the writer should carefully consider the letter's content.

A letter writer should be familiar with the protocol and regulations of the company they are writing to, as well as the terminology used in formal communication. While composing the letter, he/she should also practice being concise and exact and using a genuine attitude. Two aspects of letter preparation are involved:

- Content planning, or deciding what the transmitter intends to say to the recipient.
- Expression planning, or the manner of the content, includes vocabulary, language selection, tone, and so on.

The author of the letter should place it in the appropriate setting. The accompanying guidelines or requirements for composing business letters often alluded to as the "business letter composing C's" must be taken into consideration.

1. **Completion**: An official letter should be comprehensive. There cannot be any facts omitted. All of the recipient's queries that come to mind should be addressed. Take into account the letter below:

Essential information, such as the insurance number, kind of insurance, title, when the insurance first went into effect, and others, were omitted from the letter, delaying the recipient's ability to take action. Writing credit numbers, user ID numbers, the PNR code, the date the seat was purchased, the travel date, and other pertinent information is required when managing contact with an institution or a ticket inquiry, for instance. The writer needs to make a distinct table of each of the pertinent elements while composing the statement. Furthermore, she/he must make sure that the statement's body contains them. She/he must ascertain whether his/her letter fully addresses all the queries that the recipient is expected to have.

2. The next rule of business statement composing is correctness. The author must initially check that the information is accurate. He/she needs to confirm the data and details. Before recording the facts on paper, he/she must confirm them. Secondly, he/she must be flawless in his adherence to the rules of letter

composing. Lastly, he/she needs to proofread the content for typos, grammatical flaws, duplicates that aren't essential, and punctuation faults. Concise forms & telegraphic composing, which ought to be ignored when composing a letter, have been introduced by SMS and E-writing.Improper details, improper claims, and unsuitable manner not just leave a negative impact on the listener yet also damage the image and integrity of the firm one is speaking on behalf of.

3. **Clarity:** Business communications should be understandable upon initial reading.The presenter should make an effort to foresee what the recipient would desire to learn and should convey his/her statement in a style that the recipient can easily understand. The letter's goal and the user's motivations for delivering it should be made clear. To prevent conflict or confusion, the language should be straightforward and the information should be self-explanatory.The letter's intended message is ruined by prolonged, convoluted phrases, poor word selection, and an aggressive demeanour. Clarity may be added to any communication by picking the intended audience, utilizing concise phrases, and properly selecting the terms.

4. **Clarity:** The letter creator needs to be succinct. The goal should be to communicate more with fewer terms. The presenter should rewrite the initial text by switching out low-information terms for high-content terms and tightening up loose constructs. For instance, to provide our cherished consumers with the finest service feasible, I am authorized to provide this proposal while bearing your interests in mind.We are providing this to our cherished clients with their finest intentions in view, to restate this. The presenter should refrain from being wordy and repetitious; unclear statements and terms should be swapped out for clear ones; using one term rather than 2 would promote brevity. Education can help you develop brevity.

5. Regard and Courtesy: Companies want to build connections based on respect and courtesy, and this may be done via a human connection. The communicator might build a personal connection with the reader by stressing the nice and the beneficial and concentrating on you rather than I or us. Being polite has a high return on investment.

The letter should be written in a compassionate and polite tone throughout. If the circumstances call for it, it may change and turn hostile or demanding. Yet it's preferable to refrain from being harsh or offensive.

Courtesy: By communicating with someone politely, one gains their regard. A polite tone shows the sender's kindness and encourages a good reaction from the recipient. Additionally, it promotes a positive perception of the sender's person or business. One should develop tact, consideration, and appreciation. The letter must use respectful, cordial language.

How the business letter should look?

Almost as important as content preparation is selecting the appropriate visual effect. A well-written letter loses its impact if it is poorly delivered. When writing a letter composer cannot stand to ignore the accompanying issues:

a. Quality Stationery.

b. the appropriate division of space among the parts of a business letter.

c. a tidy look and appropriate format

d. typed, if at all practicable;

e. if handmade, legible, and adhering to all fundamental writing conventions.

f. using grammar, spelling, and punctuation correctly

g. clear foolscap sheet,

h. a suitable font (if computer-based),

i. a cleanly and suitably folded sheet,

j. a suitable envelope completes the list and

k. properly addressed, ideally in the middle of the envelope.

Gomti Nagar,
Lucknow.
29th April, 2008

The Managing Director
Quest Consultancy
Lekhraj Marg
Lucknow

Sir

I hereby resign from the post of Assistant Marketing Manager and request you to relieve me after the expiry of one month notice period, that is, from 29th July, 2008.

As you know, I joined this company seven years ago as Junior Marketing Executive and was promoted only three year back. My career growth is slow and I feel I am stagnating in this job. With my experience and qualifications, I believe, I would be able to get elsewhere a better position and a more congenial atmosphere according to my profession.

I, must, however, assure you that I have enjoyed working in the organization. The experience gained here would help me make a more valuable and satisfying contribution to this profession. In the end I would like to thank you and colleagues for the courtesy and consideration shown to me during my stay here.

Yours faithfully
Anshuman Singh

Figure 39: Example of resignation letter

Chapter -2

Memorandum and Report Writing

Memorandum (Memo)

A memorandum is a brief piece of documentation that a member of an organization uses to connect with other members of the organization. A memo is a message intended to aid recollection, according to the dictionary definition of the term. Interior communications involving managers and employees are done through memos. It is never distributed beyond the company.

The goal of composing a memo

Memos might be employed for certain formal communications. Memos have been typically employed for the following purposes:

1. To provide scheduled information.

2. For generating regular reports.

3. To communicate organizational transformation.

4. For giving the workers instructions.

5. To confirm a phone-based judgment.

6. For requesting specific, specialized facts.

7. For composition advice.

A caution from management may occasionally be necessary for a misbehaving worker. To caution means to alert someone to a bad outcome. Whenever all other options have failed, it is crucial to issue a warning to the negligent worker. Administration only employs this method of communication when it is necessary to restrain or alter particular actions that conflict with corporate rules and discipline.

A worker who has committed an offense is first informed by the administration. If the worker doesn't modify her or his actions as requested, the administration will deliver a gently spoken caution. Management's methods of disciplining a worker range from reprimands to warnings. This offers the misbehaving worker a chance to make amends. The worker receives a written warning if he/she chooses to disregard this chance and continues acting improperly. In Indian slang, this written caution is also referred to as a memo. Any memo could constantly be responded to by the worker. Typically, the worker's employment is removed following the issuance of 2 such memos. The worker is made conscious of the significance of his/her offense by a handwritten memo, and he/she has the option of changing his/her ways. A written letter provides the administration the chance to compile evidence or a complaint sheet over such a worker. This makes it easier to pursue any further legal proceedings against him/her.

Perks of memo

1. **Affordable:** This method of communication is affordable since it is passed from person to person within the organization.

2. **Convenient**: Because all headings, including those for data, people, and other categories, are often presented in a uniform style, memos are easy to compose and understand. Comparatively speaking, memoranda are easier to write, send, and comprehend than letters.

3. **For future use:** Memos are typically kept on electronic discs or in workplace folders. They can therefore be employed as a resource in the long term.

4. **Speedy:** Memos guarantee an efficient and speedy movement of content in every way. The occupied CEOs and staff can communicate with one another through note swaps without disrupting their daily activities.

5. Improving accountability: Because memos serve as recordings of information and judgments, they improve accountability. Hence, certain organizations choose memos over the telephone or spoken communication, even for minor occasions and requests.

The format of the memo

As opposed to a letter, a memo has a distinct structure. As the memos are frequently passed from one unit or worker to the other, it is crucial to include the names of both the sender and the reader, as well as their respective designations and departments. Citation numbers are also necessary.

Every memo must have the terms "From" and "To." There is no greeting, and neither the subscribing information nor a complimenting closure is written after the narrator's sign. The message is as concise as it can be, clear in writing, and correctly dated.

When thinking about the tone, the following 3 things should be retained in mind:

1. Who will read this memo?

3. The business in the house design,

2. the memo's topic content, and

3. A memo may not be overly official, nor must it seem so casual as to lose any sense of seriousness.

ABC Motors Pvt. Ltd.
Lucknow

Date:..............

Office Memorandum

Ref. Number : 592/20.....
To   : Puneet Mohan
               Administration
From   : Rajeev Srivastava, D.G.M.
Subject   : Reading newspapers and magazines in office hours.

I appreciate your interest in the rapidly changing political scene in the country. But would you please confine your reading of newspapers and magazine before, or after office hours sitting in the comfort of your drawing room?

You will agree that maintaining office decorum is of utmost importance for the welfare of the organization.

Figure 40: Example of inner-office memo

Report writing

An organized display of facts about an incident, a course of activity, or a particular commercial operation is known as a report. It is a textual record of outcomes, developments, traits, circumstances, developments, or the evaluation of documents. An essential administrative resource for formulating decisions is a report. A report conveys facts from a source to a recipient who requires it.

An oral report seems straightforward and simple to deliver. It might involve sharing an opinion or an insight. However, a written report is usually preferable since

1. A report given orally may be rejected at any moment. However, a report in writing is a lasting record.

2. Oral reports frequently lack specificity. The writer strives to be exact and exact when writing a report.

3. A report that is written could be consulted again.

4. Less transmission-related distortion

Different forms of business reports

A) According to the requirements of the law

1. **Informal reports:** These are composed in the style of letters that are sent from one individual to the other. Informal reports often don't adhere to any established format or process. There is no set order among them. As per the firm's comfort and needs, they are constructed. These analyses could be instructive or directional.

2. **Official reports:** A formal report includes one that is created in a predetermined format and delivered to a certain authority in line with predetermined steps.

   - **Statutory:** It is a report referred to as a "statutory report" if it is written in the format and guidelines established by law.

   - **Non-statutory:** It is a formal report that is generated to assist the administration in formulating policy or making other crucial decisions yet is not mandated by any legislation are referred to as non-statutory reports.

B) A report could be classified as regular or special depending on how frequently it is released.

1. **Regular or usual reports:** They are created and delivered in regular, predetermined schedules as part of business as usual. They might be sent in every day. Bank branch managers often report to the main office on the volume of business done within a specific period.

2. **Special reports:** These focus on a specific event or circumstance. Special reports include topics like whether it would be a good idea to establish a fresh branch or whether there is employee unrest in a specific branch. Special reports cover issues that don't come up often.

C) A report may be educational depending on its role. A report is informative if it only provides information that is relevant to a problem or circumstance.

On the contrary, it might be categorized as analytic, interpreting, or exploratory if it examines the data, draws conclusions, and makes recommendations.

D) We could conduct a discussion about the topic being discussed based on its character.

- Report that identifies the issue

- Report on a fact-finding

- Report on performance

- Technical report and so on.

E) Depending on how many people are keen on participating in the report-writing process, we could have:

- Individual reports;

- Reports from panels or sub-panels.

Qualities of the report

An effective report should be

- succinct and accurate,
- accurate,
- clear,
- relevant, and
- reader-focused

Purpose of the report

1. It provides the administration with facts.

2. It keeps track of information and poll or research findings for subsequent use.

3. It offers essential facts to the general public, lenders, consumers, and investors.

4. It offers suggestions for application in the future.

Report writing: key principles

1. The report must be directed to a specific person or group, such as the Chief Executive or the Board of Directors.

2. It must have a brief, distinct title that makes it obvious what the report is about.

3. The report must include the word of reference so that it becomes evident why it is necessary, as reports are typically written on the demand or advice of a recipient.

4. The content of the report must be organized, logically sequenced, and should have headings.

5. Any suggestions must be indicated to draw emphasis to them right away. The official in charge of it might endorse it, and the date must be included.

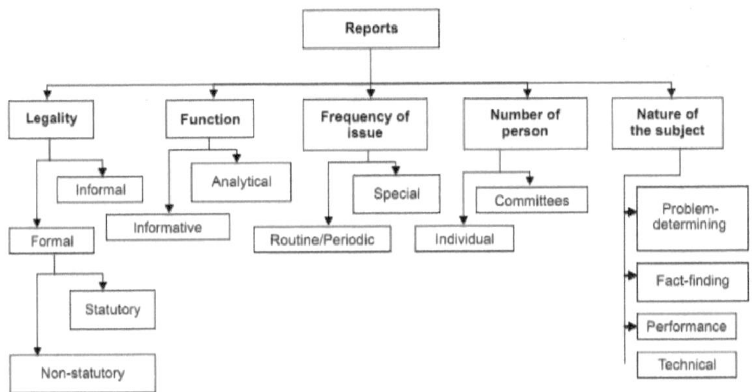

Figure 41: Flow chart report types

Preparation of a report

The 5 phases listed below should be followed when writing a report.

- looking into the information's sources;

- taking records;

- examining the facts;

- creating an overview; and

- Composing a report

Structure of the report

1) Letter format: Letter format is advised for informal reports. The header or topic, date, location, greeting, body, complementing closure, and sign make up the bulk of the document.

The letter's core is subsequently separated into:

(i) **Introduction:** It describes the scope of the research and the criteria of reference. (It mentions the issue with the word of reference plus pertinent facts.)

(ii) **Outcomes:** The trial's conclusions are discussed in the following sentences.

(iii) **The recommendation** makes sense in light of the conclusions in the final paragraph of the section.

2) **Memorandum:** It is more straightforward than a formal letter. At the very top, the date is stated. The identity of the individual to whom the report is written, the identity of the author, and the report's content are then listed. The content itself and the conclusion come following. Similar to a letter, a report's content is broken up into sections with headings and subheadings.

3) **The letter-text combo format:** The letter-textual mixture format is typically used for lengthy reports. A full report in this format is broken down into 3 main sections: -

(i) Introduction sections

■ **Letter of presentation or transmission**

A letter of transmission is a standard letter used to provide a report from its author to its recipient. It offers everlasting documentation of the transference, displays the date when the report was filed, including the name and title of the presenter, authorized the report, and invites reader feedback. The report's focus mentions the author's informational sources and emphasizes unique aspects.

■ Cover

In essence, it offers the report a tidy look and safeguards the content against destruction. The name and address of the corporation are printed on some companies' cover pages, which are produced in printed form. Other than that, it includes the study's title, date, number, and classification—such as confidential, highly classified, and so on.

■ Title

The title page includes the report's topic, the writer's name, the name of the authorities for whom the report was produced, the month and year it was completed, and other information.

■ Preface

The majority of the detail regarding the report's features is contained in the opening, which also occasionally mentions the report's shortcomings. Before presenting a report to the viewers, it contains prefatory statements.

■ Acknowledgement

Make sure to accurately list the names of the people and companies who assisted to prepare the report, except if you have already done so elsewhere. In acting so, we speak and act with sincerity and courtesy.

■ Table of contents

The table makes it clear what distinct items you should include in the report and where they might be referenced or clarified. It is recommended that the relevant page number come after the information.

■ **List of figures/table**

A thorough and methodically created report might include illustrations, a list of charts, images, or diagrams, along with the page number where each might well also be found.

■ **Abstract or synopsis**

The viewer can quickly understand the report's main points thanks to the synopsis. The report is summarized in an abstract. In actuality, the abstract clarifies the purpose of the report and its importance. In contrast, a summary is a condensed version of the complete report. A summary is longer compared to an abstract.

(ii) The Report's body

■ **Introduction**

An introduction of a report serves to convey the topic to the audience.

•Background information, both historical and technological.

• How the information is organized.

• The study's scope, including its qualifications and restrictions.

• Approval of the reference terms and report.

• Special terminology and symbol descriptions, if there are any.

The purpose and theme of the report must be clearly stated, and there must be sufficient background information to explain to the viewer why the issue was deemed important enough to investigate.

■ **Methodology**

Each report that does not identify where and how the information was gathered is not regarded to be acceptable. There are 2 types of data: Primary and secondary. Material that is employed for the initial time by the author is considered primary, whereas data that has already been employed elsewhere is considered secondary.

■ Analysis or Discussion

The report's major portion or part is this. Interpretations, analysis, and assessment are all included in this section. Using sections and subsections, it carefully describes the several facets of the problem. This section's primary goal is to organize the presentation of data, evaluate its importance, and outline its investigation and any subsequent findings. It has graphs, statistics, charts, and more.

■ Outcomes

This section includes a presentation of the anticipated outcome of the inquiry, along with a discussion of each component's benefits and drawbacks. Each approach has an in-depth justification. Outcomes are organized and displayed in a logical or sequential order. It might contain images, charts, graphs, tables, infographics, etc. depending on the section.

■ Conclusions

The study essentially concluded at this point, therefore it's important to properly describe the important findings. Nothing additional must be added at this point; all findings should be validated by the prior work. If they are numerous, they can be listed in descending order of significance.

■ Suggestions

The conclusion and suggestion ought to be included in the same part if the report is brief since they are interconnected. However, in lengthy reports, this method causes uncertainty in the viewer's thinking and renders it challenging for the author to clarify. The suggestion recommends a plan of action to be followed and details the outcomes. It ought to be expressly stated in the end and serve as the basis for decision-making.

Note: Students are often confused about the finding, conclusion and recommendation.

Findings are factual and verifiable statements of what happened or what was found.

Conclusions are your own ideas that you deduce from your finding.

Recommendations are what you want done.

Figure 42: A small note for report writing

(iii) Final Matters

■ References/Bibliography

By describing them at the closing of the report, the researcher gives acknowledgment to the relevant contributor in this area. When there are few references, they are listed at the bottom of the following section where they are utilized as footnotes. Additionally, if there are several of them, a distinct document should be attached.

■ Glossary

A description of each technological term in the report's glossary is provided. Furthermore, as with the list of references, if there are few references, annotations are added; however, if there are enough, a distinct glossary part is included.

■ Appendices

It includes graphs, charts, and analytical tables that are necessary to complement the report's primary body. However, such information can be securely omitted by the viewer without affecting their comprehension of the report's facts. Additionally, the appendices must contain the confirming or relevant proof and papers if the reader wants to review them in depth.

Chapter - 3

Employing the Case Study Approach

Describe case study

A case study comprises a representation of a real-world administrative scenario where a choice had to be taken or an issue had to be fixed. Aspects of the scenario may be exactly as reported but have been covered up for privacy concerns. Several case studies have been structured so that the viewer assumes the role of the manager, whose duty it is to decide how to address the issue. Nearly always, a choice should be taken in a case study, even if that choice is to accomplish nothing and leave things as they are.

A learning approach employing the case approach

In contrast to the classroom technique, during which the lecturer communicates and the learners observe and make records, the case approach of study involves direct dialogue between teachers and students. The teacher acts as a mentor instead of merely a speaking head while teaching using the case approach, which allows pupils to educate themselves. Learners' collective, collaborative efforts are emphasized as a key component of education.

The initial step in preparing allocated cases is done through the learners, and the teacher uses this study as the foundation for a discussion in class. Learners pick up skills like problem-solving, making judgments, and oral debating, frequently unintentionally. By employing this strategy, they develop their ability to conceptualize issues from an executive's point of view. In programs that heavily rely on the case approach, a sizable chunk of the participant's assessment might conceptualize depending on their involvement in case conversations in class, while a sizable part might depend on their written case studies. Due to these factors, employing the case approach can be exceedingly time-consuming for both learners and teachers.

Different kinds of case study

1. An illustrated case study analyses a condition by using 1 or 2 examples to explain an area. This aids in the interpretation of other data, particularly when investigators have cause to suspect that program viewers lack sufficient program knowledge. This case study helps viewers understand the unknown and provides a shared language for discussing the subject. To keep viewers interested, the selected domain must represent significant variances and have a limited range of cases. A limited range of instances is chosen for this form of case study to maintain reader interest. Visual proof is frequently used in data, research that considers the quality and interpretation of the data, and reporting that uses self-contained, independent stories or explanations.

Figure 43: Six different types of the case study (illustrated, exploratory, critical instance, implementation program, program effect, and cumulative)

2. The case study procedure is streamlined in an exploratory case study. They may be carried out by investigators before starting a significant investigation. The exploratory case study aids in formulating queries, choosing assessment concepts, and creating indicators when there is a great deal of ambiguity around program activities, objectives, and outcomes. They protect financial investments in more extensive investigations as well.

3. The case study of critical instances looks at one or more places to accomplish one or more goals. Examining a scenario of special relevance while showing little to no concern in generalization is a relatively common utilization. This approach is especially suitable for responding to cause-and-effect queries regarding the problematic situation. The biggest flaw in this research is the assessment question's poor description. Investigating the fundamental issues in a request is vital to the proper use of the case study of critical instances.

4. Implementation program: When execution constraints are a problem, this kind of case study might be helpful. Longitudinal reports that detail what has occurred over time might provide a framework for understanding a conclusion about execution variations. In either scenario, investigators should properly craft the assessment queries for their client while aiming toward generalization.

5. The case study of program effects could assess the impacts of initiatives and offer conclusions regarding the causes of achievement or loss. Similar to the case study on program implementation, the assessment queries typically call for generalization, and for a substantially varied program, it might be challenging to provide appropriate answers while maintaining a reasonable number of locations. Yet there are methodical answers to this issue. One method entails initially performing the case study at locations selected for their

representativeness, after which the results are confirmed by looking over administration statistics, earlier studies, or a poll. Another answer entails first trying alternative approaches. Investigators might subsequently perform case studies in particular areas after recognizing results of particular relevance to maximize the value of the data.

6. The case study of cumulative combines data from various places that were gathered over time. It could have a retrospective emphasis, gathering data from previous studies, or a future perspective, planning a sequence of inquiries at various future points in time. Prospective cumulation and retrospective cumulation both enable generalization without the expense and time of undertaking several novel case studies, as well as without an unmanageably high volume of ongoing cases. The methods used to ensure adequate comparison and quality as well as to aggregate the data make up the "cumulative" portion of the approach. The case survey approach and backfill procedures are characteristics of this case study. The case survey approach is employed to aggregate outcomes. The latter facilitates retrospective cumulation by helping authors provide material that enables the application of case studies that would normally be inadequately comprehensive.

Ways to perform a case study

While there is no single, universal "Case Approach" or method, most techniques concur that a case study should be approached using a set of standard stages. Naturally, many teachers may advise you to approach situations in various ways; this is a facet of lifestyle and would also be a portion of functioning for other people. This variation is advantageous as it would demonstrate many approaches to decision-making. Users would receive the following in advance (typically a week before):

1. the case study.

2. Frequently, certain leading queries must be addressed, and

3. (Occasionally) certain reading tasks that are somewhat related to the case's topic.

There are three parts to the job you must do to complete the case:

1. What does one do to get ready for the class discussion?

2. What happens during the case discussion in school? and

3. Is anything else necessary after the class discussion?

Users must complete all 3 steps for optimal efficiency. Here are the parts in the correct order. Soon, we'll go into greater depth about them.

Before the discussion

1. Go through the assigned readings (if required).

2. Get familiarized with the case by using the Shorter Cycle Method.

3. To examine the situation, utilize the long cycle method.

4. Typically, one's suggestions would be discussed in group sessions.

5. Summarize the case (if needed).

During discussion

1. At some point throughout the class discussion, typically at the teacher's encouragement, somebody would initiate the conversation.

2. Pay close attention and make notes. Keep an eye out for assumptions. Make sure they are expressed adequately.

3. Participate in the conversation. Your participation is significant, and it probably counts toward the course assessment.

Following the class discussion

After class, go over all the information. Take note of the main idea and the way the case would be managed while taking into account any restrictions.

Preparation for a case study

Whenever starting to create a case study, it assists to establish a strategy because the amount of material and problems to be addressed could originally appear fairly overwhelming. An excellent place to begin is with what follows.

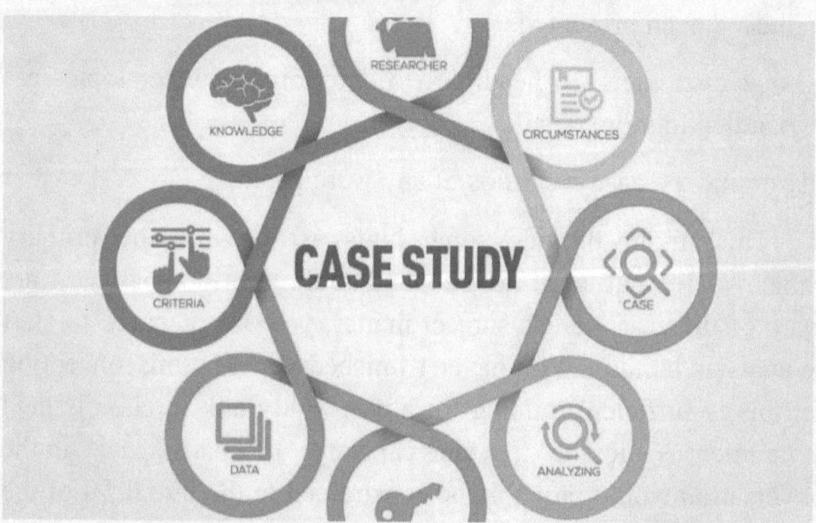

Figure 44: How to investigate a case study?

Phase 1-The Short Cycle Method

1. Study the case thoroughly. One might simply desire to study the initial few and final sections at this point if the case is lengthy. After that, one ought to be able to

2. Respond to the accompanying queries:

(i)   What is the decision-position developer's scope of responsibility in this instance?

(ii) What does the difficulty, threat, potential, or source of stress seem to be, and what does that seem to mean for the company?

(iii) Why is the decision-maker presently concerned and why has the problem emerged?

(iv) By what deadline must the decision-maker determine, settle, take action, or deal with the matter? What is the situation's level of emergency?

3. Check out the displays to examine the figures that have indeed been presented.

4. Look over the case headlines to determine whether topics are handled in more detail.

5. Examine the case scenarios, if any were given.

This might provide some hints as to what the primary problems are that need to be handled. Presently that users are aware of the case study's subject matter, you are prepared to start the analysis method. You haven't finished yet! The misconception that this is sufficient training for a case study talk in class is held by numerous learners. One's capacity to participate in the conversation would probably be constrained to the initial 1/4 of the given class duration if this represented the amount of the research. Utilizing the subsequent stage, you must continue to build your case. One can get an idea of how much effort would be required to adequately plan the case study by using the shorter-cycle approach, which is among the main goals.

Phase 2: The long-cycle approach

Currently, there are five aspects to the activity:

1. Carefully studying the case, followed by.

2. Examining the case, second.

Examine the accompanying parts when users are thoroughly studying the case study:

1. Establishes the scenario in the introductory paragraph.

2. Background data, including facts on the market, the company, the goods, the competition, the economy, and anything else of note.

3. Particular (workable) field of involvement: combined, advertising, economics, operational, or HR.

4. The particular issue or decision(s) at hand.

5. The decision-potential maker's options, whereby the case might or might not specify.

6. The activity, any restrictions or constraints, and the seriousness of the circumstance are all outlined in the end.

Many case studies would adhere to this structure, yet not all would. Understanding the circumstance and the choices that would require to be taken in full is the goal here. Note the observations, take time, and do not lose sight of your goals. The problem assessment process consists of 7 phases.

1. **Cautiously and properly examine the case:** To properly comprehend whatever occurring in a particular instance, it is essential to do so. To acquire a general understanding of the field, the business, the individuals, and the circumstance, you might wish to peruse the case pretty rapidly the initial time. Re-read the case carefully and take details as you proceed.

2. **Identify the main issue:** Often situations would have multiple difficulties or issues. Differentiate the most significant difficulties from the less significant ones. Evaluate associated issues in the operational domains after establishing what seems to be a significant fundamental issue (for instance, personnel,

advertising, finance, etc.). Identifying difficulties in the operational areas that constitute the duty of topmost administration might be helpful.

3. **Specify the company's objectives:** Discordances between an organization's objectives and its performance might serve to emphasize the issues found in phase 2 even more. Finding the company's objectives would, at the least, serve as a guideline for the subsequent assessment.

4. **Determine the restrictions on the dilemma:** The restrictions might restrict the options the company has for answers. Financial restrictions, a shortage of increased manufacturing capability, staffing shortages, fierce competition, connections involving vendors and consumers, and other issues are examples of typical restraints. When making a solution suggestion, restrictions must be taken into account.

5. **Include all viable solutions:** The list must contain all viable solutions that could address the issue(s) that were discovered in phase 2. Come up using creative ideas by using your imagination. You might be capable to offer superior ideas even though they are already provided in the case.

6. **Decide which option is best:** Consider each option in the context of the facts at hand. A sound resolution to the matter must be obvious if the 5 procedures were properly followed. Avoid the urge to do this stage before the case analysis has finished. You will likely overlook crucial information, get the issue wrong, or ignore what might be the finest possible option answer.

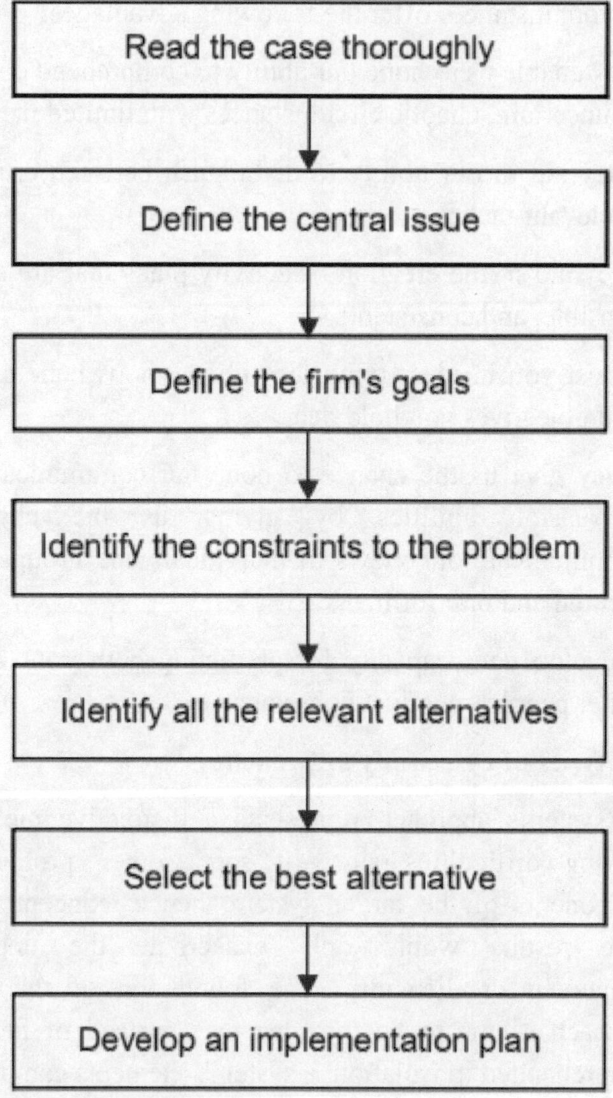

Figure 45: Process of case study analysis

7. Create an execution strategy: The last phase in the assessment is to create a strategy for successfully putting your choice into action. Even a really wise idea might go wrong if you do not have a strategy for how to execute it. Do not skip this action. Since there are occasions when you must describe to others how to carry out the decision.

In conclusion, instances offer the following advantages:

- They enable us to hone our ability to comprehend coherently in uncertain, chaotic circumstances with limited facts;

- They aid in our ability to distinguish between crucial and irrelevant facts;

- They aid in the creation of activity plans that are succinct, sensible, and consistent;

- Assist you in identifying the subconscious beliefs, values, and objectives you hold dear;

- They give us the chance to hone our communication and persuasion abilities by giving us the chance to communicate our views to individuals and groups in both written and oral form.

- Develop your capacity for predicting both your own and other people's conduct consequences.

Different types of case study approaches

1. The systems approach represents a distinctive method for tackling difficulties since it sees some "problems" as components of the larger system; hence, concentrating on these results would only exacerbate the undesirable component or difficulty. The foundation of the systems approach seems to be the idea that, instead of being best comprehended in isolation, a system's elements can indeed be comprehended most in the setting of their connections with other organizations. Understanding the component in connection to the total is the sole method to completely comprehend why a difficulty or component arises and continues. By investigating the connections and reactions among the various components that make up a system as a whole, a systems approach aims to comprehend that system. The use of a systemic approach in a case study demonstrates

how the viewer must take other factors into account when examining or addressing a specific instance.

2. The case study's behavioural approach uses the methodologies and strategies of social sciences to examine human action, including anthropology, psychology, sociology, and social psychology. The readers collect and examine data objectively to examine many facets of human action. With this method, the reader assesses the case in terms of personal variations. They attempt to resolve the issue by taking into account not just the material aspects of the situation yet also human conduct. Since the halo phenomenon, biasing occasionally results.

3. The decision-making approach entails picking a plan of activity from a wide range of options. This study was carried out by outlining numerous potential answers to a given issue, each of which was then carefully considered before being selected.

4. An improved variant of the choice method is the strategic approach. In the context of a strategic approach, one must determine the option by taking into account the purposes and goals of a specific body or company. This method of thinking is appropriate for long-term solutions.

While investigating a specific issue, there is no universal rule for selecting any of the aforementioned ways. Most readers are concerned with all issues that have to do with systems, decisions, and strategic approaches in addition to action.

Dos of case presentation

1. Be thoroughly familiar with the case before you start your case study assessment.

2. Allow adequate time for you to complete the case study assessment. You do not desire to go too quickly.

3. Be truthful in the assessments. Keep your ideas and personal difficulties from influencing your decision.

4. Think analytically, not descriptively.

5. Edit the work for errors.

Don'ts of case presentation

1. Try acting devil's advocate and putting oneself in the other individual's perspective rather than giving up at the first apparent solution.

2. Avoid attempting to fix all of the identified issues. It is preferable to focus on a small number of issues properly rather to attempt to tackle too much.

3. Try to prevent forming rash judgments or equating signs with issues.

4. Instead of writing a message to a friend, write in a professional style appropriate for academic study.

Unit- VI

Presentation Skills and Communication

Chapter- 1

Presentation Skills

Presentation

Presentations represent a serious subject. Its goal is to give a viewpoint or enlighten, clarify, and convince the listener. It might present a commodity, clarify a procedure, or recount an encounter. At a lecture, workshop, or corporate event, it is presented to a limited, educated group. The audience then has the opportunity to ask queries.

With certain formal education and experience, presentation skills could be built and nurtured. As with giving a speech, preparation must be completed in 4 phases:

1. Learning about the setting, or you can state the various presenting aspects, and where the presentation will be made.

2. Creating the content and necessary graphics.

3. Taking good care of one's looks and manners.

4. Test out your presenting approach.

Figure 46: Effective presentation skills for business communication

Essential factors of presentation

1. **The location:** One would feel more at ease if one is acquainted with the area. However, don't neglect to inspect the space and all necessary materials a few mins ahead of the presentation. One should put attempt to become acquainted with the venue, the seating layout, and the speaker's posture if it is outdoors. Examine the visual aids in detail. Take note of its location and projections.

2. **The coordinator:** Do your best to learn as much as you can regarding the organizer, the firm's name, and the names of its key personnel.

3. **The context:** You must be aware of the context where you will be giving your presentation, such as a corporate conference, workshop, or lecture.

4. **Check the amount** of period you have accessible in advance. One must adhere strictly to the time limit.

5. **Extra speakers Determine the other speakers.** Will there be people representing competitor companies? What role does their company hold? Regardless of whether they are there, be cautious not to say anything negative about opponents.

6. **The viewer:** The presentation should take the viewer's demands and inclinations into consideration. The viewer's characteristics will determine the speech's topic and tone. Be careful with the terminology you employ in the presentation; avoid making any potentially offensive references. Among the elements to consider is the viewer's age range. The below could offer a hint:

(a) Kids enjoy hearing tales and are drawn to dramatic performances.

(b) University and high school learners prefer to be considered adults. They are receptive to fresh concepts, and value an honest, clear perspective yet are also inclined to be analytical, and they anticipate a well-prepared speech with relevant information.

(c) Younger adults have the most sophisticated demographic; they have a diverse spectrum of interests and a forward-thinking outlook. They enjoy novel initiatives and concepts yet are also quite critical.

(d) The middle-aged population is conservative and is less likely to readily embrace fresh concepts. Individuals possess significant life expertise and understanding yet might not be as excited regarding modifications or fresh concepts. They hear with attention yet are not as quick to adopt.

(e) The majority of the time, senior adults are curious about current events and fresh developments. They also enjoy being brought back to the past. What level of education and income does the population have? Whatever generation group's extremely educated viewers are particularly critical. As a group, the wealthy are opposed to societal reform.

Presentation design

For each min you discuss, you require an hour of preparation. The most crucial step is to choose your words carefully, gather the necessary data, and provide them with a suitable structure. It should be coherent and possess a clear progression from one idea to the following. Include the location, the introduction, and the closing words in your notes for the entire presentation. After that, refine, revise, and perfect it until you have a strong presentation that fits the time allotted.

- **Length:** The session moves along at an approximate rate of 100 words per min. Give a speech to determine your speaking pace. A 2-min speech can be composed on an A4 size page with 1 and a half spacing line and 12 font sizes. 400–500 words make up a presentation that lasts 4-5 mins.

- **A speech should sound conversational**. Employ simple lines so the audience may understand. Make sure the language you employ is appropriate for your viewers. Be formal in your approach. Communicating in a formal context differs from communicating in a societal or personal context in terms of formality.

- **Humour:** Make sure one can laugh without getting awkward or looking ridiculous. Humour ought to be unforced, carefree, pleasurable, and pertinent to the subject. No audience must feel embarrassed or offended by it.

Presentation outline preparation

An agenda for a presentation serves a similar purpose as one for a textual report: it assists you in structuring your content to have the most possible influence on your listeners. Develop your blueprint in steps to achieve efficient establishment:

- **Describe your core concept and intent:** Make periodic checks as you create your outline to ensure that the topics, structure, linkages, and title are relevant to your goal and key concept.

- **Arrange your main ideas and supporting details:** To maintain the pace of the one main notion you wish to communicate in each significant statement, describe each of them as a full sentence. Furthermore, ensure the ideas are presented in a logical and efficient sequence by paying attention to the sequence.

- **Determine your opening, middle, and conclusion:** Beginning using the body, assign a rank to every significant point and subpoint based on its position in your design. Then list the key elements for your opening and closing.

- **Display your contacts.** The changes you intend to utilize to go from one section to the following should be written out in whole sentences. In the speech's content, don't forget to use more transitions between key topics.

- **Indicate your resource:** When creating your bibliography, ensure it is clear to read, adheres to a standard structure, and contains all the information required to distinguish your numerous resources. Be ready to cite important resources during your discussion as necessary.

- **Select a title:** Not every presentation or talk has a title. A headline, nevertheless, can be helpful if somebody else will deliver your work or market it beforehand.

- **Reduce points and changes to a few crucial utterances:** Pick words that would help you recall the details of every point so you could communicate clearly. Additionally, you might wish to use whole lines to move between key topics or at important parts of your opening or conclusion.

Figure 47: Visual aids and their importance

- **Including delivery, and cues:** Make a note of the locations in the design during practice when you intend to halt for highlights, talk more gradually, utilize a visual, etc.

Visual tools

They are used by the presenter to convey information in a structured manner, demonstrate points using diagrams, and display data. The viewers can view a graphic overview of the topics and receive visual reinforcement for whatever they have heard. Either one or multiple of the accompanying sophisticated visual tools are appropriate:

1. You can put up posters in practically any place. Despite being outdated, advertising professionals who travel to rural communities have discovered this to be a fairly reliable strategy.

2. A flip chart needs support or an easel. The most effective application is interactive displays. One can display thoughts from the crowd on it. Then concentrate on it while the people are present. The audience members enjoy seeing their suggestions recorded during the lecture.

3. Overhead projectors (OHP) are highly common and widely accessible. Use high-quality transparency for making slides. Insert no more than six lines on a slide. Make your writing or typing legible to the entire audience.

4. If accessible, PPT projection can indeed be employed. Don't complicate the slides. Steer clear of motion or colour. Audio should not be used to animate the slides. The presentation should make good use of visuals. Properly design them to highlight a topic with an illustration, list the essential elements, or show a graph or diagram.

Postures and appearance during the presentation

One's physical attributes and character have a significant influence.

1. Wear appropriate attire. Make sure you are properly prepared from head to toe if you are not accustomed to wearing formal attire.

2. Before you begin, the viewers take note of your body language.

3. Be in a comfortable and calm standing posture. Hold your position firmly and inhale deeply.

4. Make a hand-related decision (not in a pocket). It might be helpful to have paper, a deck of cards, and a pencil in hand.

5. Let your face relax. It can take some practice.

6. Making eye contact is crucial. In 5 secs, scan the audience as a whole. Do not forget to look everyone in the eye. If you're at ease, grin broadly and greet the day.

7. Talk loud enough to be heard by the people at the rear. The listeners become uninterested when a speaker speaks at extremes of volume.

8. The tone and amplitude of the voice must change depending on the subject and content of the talk.

9. Use breaks. Audiences become overburdened if too many statements or concepts are presented.

10. Ensure that your health is in perfect shape. You'll be active, eager, and self-assured if your health is strong. Additionally, the throat, tongue, and complete communication systems are impacted by one's physical condition and health.

Presentation rehearsal

1. Newbie presenters should practice giving presentations in person. The performance is primarily to blame for the presentation's accomplishment, regardless of how much work and thought you put into the text's preparation.

2. You can check the style and language during a rehearsal to see whether they are appropriate for conversation. It is in practice sufficient to simply read aloud. The only way to determine if the statements are comfortable and natural in speech is to try to present them to an audience.

3. Continue to practice until you feel confident using the subject in conversation.

4. Testing the timing also benefits from the practice.

5. The textual content will initially be longer than is necessary for the allotted time. You must repeat talking out loud multiple times if you're just starting.

6. After practicing in front of a mirror, any audience that may be gathered to provide constructive criticism, like a small circle of close colleagues or family.

7. Performing a whole costume rehearsal is worthwhile for your comfort.

8. Avoid memorizing speeches because it leads to dependency and can be very confusing if you miss even one word.

During presentation

If you can use the below strategies throughout the event, you can leave a positive impression:

- Don't rush the start.
- While you initially enter the room, take a second to adapt your documents and find a comfortable position. Afterward, stand up straight, take a glance slowly in all directions, create eye contact with a few listeners, customize the microphone (typically, it ought to be placed 4 to 6 cm from the mouth), and begin speaking in a loud yet confident voice.
- Give the first phrase you can remember. By recalling the opening statement, you may make eye contact and start building connections right away. You, therefore, seem more certain and competent as a result of this.

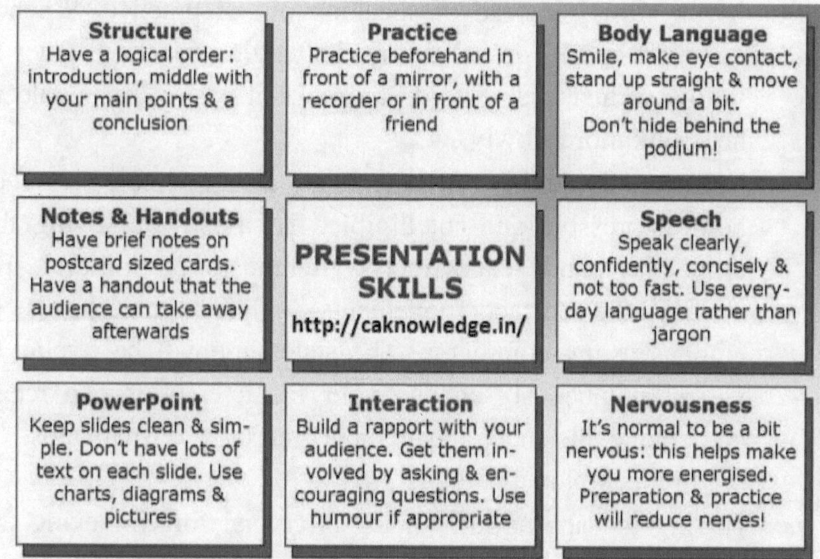

Figure 48: Key points for effective presentation

- When you have begun the talk, be especially cautious to keep eye contact with the listeners during the presentation. Choose numerous individuals from the viewer and move your eyes from one to the next. Establishing eye contact will allow you to better evaluate the image you are making.

- Regulate your tone while talking in front of a listener.

- This implies speaking in normal tones yet loud enough for everybody in the room to hear you. To increase importance, change your tone and talking rate.

- Clearing the throat or coughing regularly is prone to draw the listener's focus away from the presentation and toward the presenter. Prevent these practices that might irritate the listener. Moreover, stay away from irrelevant filler terms and phrases such as, "Well," "You know," "Uh," "Okay," and similar ones. Silence is preferable to filler words that have no real purpose. Talk loudly, precisely, and with each syllable said.

- Speak slowly instead of speaking out of practice. When a presenter speaks quickly, it is challenging for the listener to follow what is being said. To make it easier for people to hear, talk more slowly.

- Occasionally, bodily movements are used to create messages both impressive and intelligible. To avoid employing the arms and hands excessively, attempt to be mindful. By making the correct movements, employ your hands to emphasize any comments. The statement will be livelier if you simultaneously change your facial emotion. To retain and pique listener engagement, employ visual aids. If required, employ a pointer.

- Having the appropriate stance is crucial for conveying the right message. Keep your head high and your hands off the stage.

- The listeners would let you know how you are performing and if you should cut the talk short as you're presenting your message. Pay close attention to any unwanted comments made, such as speaking, giggling, shifting chairs, or other signals of displeasure.

- The listener receives multiple meanings from clothes. As a result, dress elegantly and deliberately in casual yet professional apparel. Attempt to appear just a little bit nicer than the typical audience member to appreciate them.

- To listen to a lengthy speech, the audience participants are prone to become distracted. Employ jokes to keep the viewer's attention. But if you're not good at telling jokes, don't do it as you might come across as a joke! jokes should connect to the subject matter of your talk. Never employ jokes that could offend someone because of their ethnicity, gender, race, age, or origin.

- Conclusions are highly crucial. A strong conclusion helps to uplift the listener's spirits. A strong presenter would restate their primary points and stress what they want the listener to accomplish or believe in their closing statements. Once the end is stated, the presenter shouldn't annoy the listeners by continuing to speak for a further five or ten minutes.

After completing the presentation

The majority of speeches conclude with discussions with the listeners.Even if the query and reply period begins after the presentation, one must make it known right away that you are willing to address any inquiries. You won't get distracted, lose your line of thought, or maybe lose out of time because of this preceding statement. One can successfully manage this crucial section of the presentation by using the below methods:

- Handout Materials: As soon as the session is over, pass out the materials you had previously made to the listeners.

- Promote Queries: If the scenario allows for time for queries and answers, solicit queries from the listeners. Establish a time frame for this discussion.

- Repeat Queries: Pay close attention to the query, then say it aloud to yourself and the rest of the listeners to be certain you comprehend it.

- Request Clarity: If a query is unclear or ambiguous, ask the asker to clarify it. When responding to the question, keep the entire audience in mind. Give a clear, concise response. To minimize a drawn-out discussion or further queries, maintain your response succinct and to the point.

- Recognize Your Ignorance: Do not claim to comprehend anything if you do not have the reply to a query. Instead, you openly acknowledge the truth and promise the listener that the solution will be available in a certain amount of time.

- Treat Politely: Be courteous to all questioners. Be firm, yet reasonable and polite, regardless of whether the inquiry is hostile.
- Maintain Control: Don't let one or two people dominate the query and answer session. Be sure you engage and include the whole listener. After responding to the final query, wrap up the presentation's key points and express gratitude to the listeners for the chance to speak with them. When the conference is over, take a look around and make eye contact with everyone. Lastly, collect your materials before stepping away from the stage.

Online presentation

Online presentations enable one to connect with more individuals in a shorter period, yet they call for certain planning and expertise. One should constantly back in with the audience to determine whether they possess any queries because you can't always rely on nonverbal cues to detect listener uncertainty or dissatisfaction.

Figure 49: Follow the following rules for an effective online presentation

Observe the following rules:

- Think about providing sample study resources in advance.
- If at all feasible, practice utilizing the device live.
- Keep things as simple as you can in the presentation.
- Request comments often.
- Give everybody a lot of time to interact and become accustomed to the display they are observing.

Chapter- 2

Group Communication

Meeting

Active communication is most frequently used in meetings. At different tiers in any company, it is crucial for facilitating a direct, in-person connection. Between meeting participants, they act as a means of oral communication. Nevertheless, they are accompanied by textual communication, such as announcements to gather participants, agendas to guide meetings, mins to document the events, and reports to relay facts to senior authorities.

A gathering of people to discuss strategies for completing a given task with a deadline is known as a meeting. The group's participants have similar backgrounds, shared issues, and shared passions.

The definition of a committee given by W.H. Newman is "A panel of a group of individuals particularly assigned to carry out certain administrative tasks. It demands unfettered communication between its individuals and solely operates as a group.

"A panel is a group of persons who gather by the plan to debate or take a decision about a certain issue," according to Hicks and Gullet's definition of the term. Researchers do not consider groups that happen unexpectedly or spontaneously in the concept of a committee since committee meetings follow a set agenda.

A meeting is an officially scheduled event when a problem affecting many people is discussed.

Objective

Each of the below goals could be the focus of a meeting:

• To educate and enlighten the individuals on the contents.

- To comprehend the circumstances.

- To hear the individuals' opinions.

- To allow individuals to share knowledge and suggestions.

- To encourage participants to embrace adjustments.

- To settle arguments and misunderstandings.

- To make decisions regarding issues that will have an impact on the group or company;

- To encourage members to be optimistic.

Types

(a) Depending on how it works:

1. **To provide facts:** These gatherings are held to share details and to get the speakers' and members' thoughts on it.

2. **To consult:** To make a good conclusion, the individuals are consulted during consultation meetings to get their ideas and views.

3. **To carry out ideas:** This kind of gathering is arranged to collect fresh concepts or recommendations for carrying out a task. Meetings of this kind are organized when the individuals' collaboration is necessary for the efficient completion of an assignment.

(b) According to the formality:

1. A organized meeting, such as a parliamentary session, a state assembly, a corporation investor meeting, management-employment talks, an institution senate, or a council or executive body.

2. Semi-organized meetings: These include group meetings, governing councils, general bodies of non-profit companies, advisory bodies, and administration meetings.

3. Ad hoc gatherings of workgroups, brainstorming workshops, and other forms of unstructured gatherings.

Procedure to conduct a meeting

The Latin term for knowledge is where the word "notice" gets its origin. The expression when used about a meeting denotes informing the individual in concern about the meeting. Only after giving notice to the parties involved can a meeting be legally conducted. The notice notifies individuals of the meeting's day, time, and location, as well as the topic to be addressed and, if feasible, the corresponding contributions anticipated from various meeting attendees.

Agenda

An agenda comprises a collection of subjects that will be discussed during a meeting. A well-structured agenda would aid the Chairperson in steering the meeting's business and guaranteeing that choices are made in a timely way.

ABC Motors India Ltd.
Lucknow

Notice is hereby given to all the members that the next quarterly meeting of the Board of Directors will be held on Tuesday, 12th August, 2008 at 11:30a.m. in the Board room.

Agenda

1. Conformation of Minutes of the last meeting.
2. Matters arising from the minutes.
3. Financial irregularities in Naya Nagar branch.
4. To appoint a committee for employees' welfare.
5. Any other matter with the permission of the chair.
6. Date of next meeting.

Secretary

Figure 50: Example of agenda

A draft of the agenda, as well as the meeting agenda, should be distributed to all participants. The agenda elements should be organized in sequential order. The permission of the participants is required if any changes are made to the sequence. Agenda preparation is an extremely beneficial practice:

1. The participants are better able to plan for the meeting whether it is distributed beforehand.

2. The agenda's predetermined sequence aids the chairperson in running the meeting efficiently.

3. It guarantees that only topics pertinent to that specific meeting are brought up for discussion.

4. It guarantees that each subject is adequately discussed.

5. It makes creating the minutes easier.

When creating the agenda, keep the below things in mind:

1. It must be precise and explicit.

2. It must be presented in a brief style.

3. The regular things must come first, followed by the more important issues.

4. On the agenda, any items with an identical or related nature must be presented next to one another.

5. Everything on the agenda needs to fall within the parameters of the gathering.

6. Every item on the agenda should be laid out in the context of the notice summoning the session.

Meeting minutes

The agenda's elements or themes are addressed in order, each individually throughout the meeting. Each person expresses their comments and thoughts while also debating the advantages and disadvantages of every agenda point. Eventually, they reach certain judgments or decisions, that are constantly recorded in official documents. They are known as meeting minutes.

Therefore, minutes are the authoritative recordings of the meeting's activities. In other terms, this is a summary of the conversations that were had and the conclusions that were made during the meeting. It is the responsibility of an authorized individual to explicitly record all such conversations, debates, and conclusions in writing.

The objective of taking notes is twofold:

1. to act as an official document of the meeting.

2. To act as a foundation for subsequent conversations.

The meeting minutes should include the following information:

1. The date and the meeting list.

2. A set of the people who witnessed the meeting.

3. A set of people who did not present and for whom sincerely apologize has been provided.

4. A documentation of the preceding minutes' confirmation and any revisions approved by the group.

5. The vital, essential backdrop to the subject being discussed.

6. A precise and unambiguous documentation of the resolution or conclusion made, as well as, if necessary, the people or institutions in charge of carrying out the required activity.

7. Distinct minutes must be prepared on the ethical problem when the discussion of a particular instance raises one.

Minute types

1. **Resolutions' minutes.** Just the resolutions adopted at a conference are noted in the form of minutes, and all conversations that took place before the resolutions are not mentioned.

- Decisions that fall under the purview of the panel are presented with the phrase "it was concluded that."

- On occasion, meeting participants lack the authority to decide a particular issue. They are only able to suggest their viewpoint to higher-ups who can make decisions.

- It has been decided that Sri Y.K. Yadav would be selected as the business's deputy manager having reference from August 1, 2008, and would receive monthly compensation of Rs. 40,000 along with additional incentives by corporate policies.

- It has been decided to suggest leaving out clause 7 of the MD's employment agreement because the adjustments must be accepted by him or her.

2. Narrative minutes. A study and narrative minutes have certain similarities. The resolutions adopted here are also listed along with a brief description of the conversation and ballot procedure.

Management of media

A commercial entity tries to connect with a bigger segment of society through mass communication, which is therefore further communication aspect. Both the addressor as well as the recipient are identified in a business letter. The business enterprise is the letter writer, while the recipient is a specific individual, by identity, title, organization, or legal body. In contrast, in mass media, the sender is more ambiguous or unidentified but the letter-writer, or presenter is stated. This does not imply that mass media has no intended audience. In actuality, mass communication seeks to connect with a specified target audience that is not bound to any particular location. Because of this, mass media campaigns must assure that their messages not only reach their intended viewers, yet also grab their interest. In this stage, it is critical to a company's development that it has a capable media administration division (often referred to as the PR department) to handle all of these media-related tasks.

Release of press

Press releases refer to the declaration of the significant statement or progress that a company wishes to make regarding itself to the general audience, via the media and other channels. A company might use direct, particular, or generic communication methods to convey messages. Personal writings, emails, pamphlets, reports, telephonic conversations, and direct mailings of materials are all examples of direct communications. Press releases, on the other hand, emerge crucial when the information to be delivered is of common significance to a sizable portion of society dispersed across many targeted groups. Any corporate group that desires to share the news with the audience will include in its press releases a variety of events and business-based details that the audience may be keen in learning about. Financial outcomes, product releases, achievement emphasizes, new branch offices, managerial changes, investor and user advantages, community-focused proposals, joint ventures and tie-ups, business closures, prizes and accomplishments, rankings and evaluations, study discoveries, meetings and conferences, and so on. are typical topics for press releases. Press releases don't result in any financial rewards for either the company that issues them or the media that publishes them. However, if managed correctly, they contribute to improving the company's reputation in the public eye. Press reports and press releases are two distinct things. A press report is written by a reporter who covers an occurrence independently for a publication or news institution. A corporation issues a press release when it submits content for publication that was created in-house.

Figure 51: Characteristics of the effective press release are explained below

Features of the effective press release

1. **It must be newsworthy:** This is the first and most important requirement for an effective press release. Because nobody could be eager to peruse it if it lacked significant news worth, and no publication could adopt it for publication.

2. **It must be technically accurate:** Being technically accurate is an issue of authenticity, and authenticity is a key business communication concept. Firms must also be aware that while misrepresenting the truth to deceive the audience may result in short-term gains, it will eventually reverse.

3. **It must be succinct and to the point.** Newspaper editors rarely have time to edit and trim a long announcement and create proper text, and the room is constantly at a premium. A release will have a better possibility of being incorporated if it is succinct. Press releases intended for local media should be longer than those for nationwide newspapers.

4. It ought to be written in clear, colloquial language because readers lose interest in news that is difficult to comprehend. It's as effective as not viewing it if he chooses not to peruse it or to return to it afterward. So, it is important to compose the press release.

5. It is appropriate to be published in the journal or magazine that it is being delivered. Company announcements, for instance, shouldn't be issued to publications covering sports, movies, or literature.

6. Be sure the pertinent 5Ws have indeed been properly addressed.

Who? Identify the parties engaged. Generally, names are significant.

What? Describe the significant event.

When? Specify the duration. The timeframe of the press statement is crucial as the old stuff is not news.

Where? The location is also crucial.

Why? Even while it might not necessarily be able to explain, if these facts are disclosed, they give the release more substance.

Press releases are frequently fairly brief, therefore the author will need to exercise judgment in deciding what information to convey.

In addition to this, there are certainly more considerations that should be made when planning the releases:

- Each release must include a headline that is both attractive and enticing yet not deceptive.

- The opener must be intriguing for the initial 1 or 2 paragraphs. They must also give the essence.

- Paragraphs ought to be succinct, and subcategories ought to be used if appropriate.

- A cover letter ought to be sent with each release.

Press conference

When a company has important information to share with the media and whenever a further thorough strategy and conversation are required than what can be provided by a press release, a press conference (also known as a news briefing or media conference) is arranged.

Two main motives exist for conducting a media conference. One seems to so enable a newsmaker who receives numerous inquiries from journalists and can respond to each of them instead of fielding numerous phone conversations. Other is to attempt and get media exposure for a subject that previously did not attract reporters.

One or multiple presenters might give a message during a press conference, and then journalists might ask them queries. There may be merely questioning on occasion, or there may be a message with no queries allowed. Journalists can ask queries, get responses, and quotes, and take pictures at a media conference. It is important to keep the accompanying in mind when planning press conferences:

- A week before the briefing, department editors and journalists must get an invite. A phone conversation can indeed be conducted to notify the journalists of the conference a day or 2 before the scheduled date.

- Plan your media conference for between 9 and 11 in the morning or 4 and 7 in the evening. Journalists won't have enough time to submit a narrative for the following day's daily publication if it is afterward or earlier than that.

- The media officer who is familiar with the journalists will begin and guide the event in the ideal scenario, which involves numerous participants. There ought to be 1 or 2 notable individuals there who would each make a 10-minute speech on the subject (initiative, release, contribution, inauguration, or something comparable). The facilitator will then offer the media the chance to ask any remaining queries. Overall, it must be completed in 45 minutes. Personal interviews may then be conducted afterward.

- At conferences, a "press kit" is typically given out, which includes a press release, information about the conference's organizers, a report, study findings, statements, a list of specialists, and so on. Particularly videotaped or photographic content is occasionally shared. If a media source did not provide a representative for the event, one must provide the press kit to them by messengers after the event.

- A press conference must, in the words of journalists, "yell for a headline" that is, there ought to be breaking news reported on them. Reporters will remember if a briefing is called but if there is no such information; there is a possibility that following, especially if there is breaking news, no one will attend the session. Press conferences are so common that media companies frequently dispatch inexperienced reporters to cover events.

- If at all feasible, press conferences must be replaced with press events. But there are a few technological considerations to make if one chooses to plan a press conference. These are them:

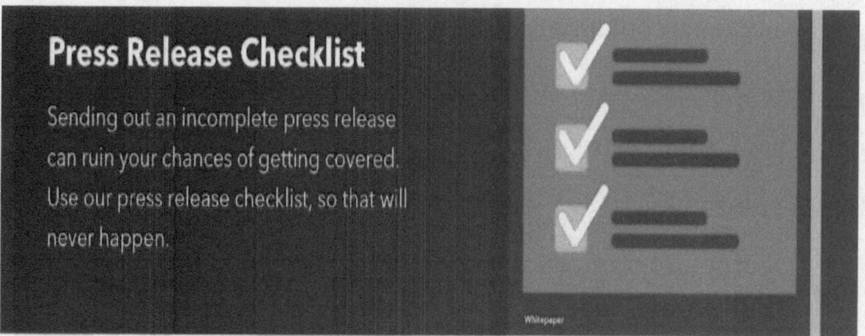

Figure 52: Press conference checklists

Checklist of the media conference

Location

- Easily reachable via public transit

- A parking spot is accessible.

- The precise location, telephone, and fax numbers

- A registration office with a staff greeted journalists at the entry

- Translating service if international journalists are anticipated

Site

- Will there be adequate outlets for TV crews?

- How robust are the fuses?

- How many guests are permitted?

- Camera station and photographers beside the journalists; Desks and seats in the appropriate numbers and positions

- Examine the heating and lighting

- Is there a photocopier on hand?

- Press kits on a table

- Members' desks with seating areas

- Where will the members approach from and exit from?

- Water cups containing water on the recipient's desk

- Is there a distinct space designated for private interviews?

- Where is the restroom?

Audio and video

- A drop-down menu containing the members' names over the firm-action logo

- LCD, video, and transparency projectors

- System of desktops, laptops, and monitors: Windows or another?

- Participatory microphones as well as a movable microphone for inquiries from the floor

- Audio equipment

- Audio, video, or photographic capturing?

While the press conference

- To keep track of attendees, maintain a sign-in form for the media and any other guests.

- Let journalists know how long the presenter will have at the start of the press conference, and be ready to end inquiries at that point.

- Limit the length of the media conference and announcements. An executive who delivers a brief announcement and answers queries will likely be more well-received by the media than one who delivers a statement for a half-hour.

- Give space for queries.

- Capture the official's comments so that they could be recorded for record forever.

- Obtain answers to open-ended queries. If a query is posed to an authority that he/she is unable to respond to, he/she ought to acknowledge the difficulty and assure the journalist that the facts will be provided before the journalist's due later that day.

After the press conference

- To ensure that it is broadly accessible, post a translation of the media briefing as quickly as you can on your website.

- Provide any interested journalists with handout resources and a translation if they were unable to present yet were interested in the topic.

- Meet all deadlines for delivering promised more information or answers to unresolved queries.

- Verify every stage of the process, then compile the observations for the upcoming conference.

Press interview

Interviews are a tool used by journalists to obtain facts and develop their articles. It is the fundamental instrument for news collecting and a fantastic way for the business to reach out to its targeted audience with its content. A company can use media interviews to promote its positive image to the viewers. Because of this, here is certain advice for media interviews:

- Never take a chance. Planning is essential for delivering messages well. Engage with your internal public relations staff or a skilled media instructor to put effort and time into practice sessions. Ask your partner, your romantic partner, or a reliable friend to grill you. Prepare yourself for difficult or aggressive queries by creating and perfecting concise, truthful, and suitable responses.

- Start modestly. Before making it huge, test out smaller locations. Trade exhibitions are an excellent place to start if you want to hold a lot of media conferences using a group of reporters who are normally rather cordial. Keep your emotions under control. Even if it's natural to feel anxious, avoid displaying anxiety or uncertainty through body language.

- Take charge of the interview. Make an assertive introduction and start the greeting to be the next one to communicate. Ask a couple of straightforward queries to the interviewer right away, like who else they've talked to and how much duration they will require. By doing this, you take control of the situation and demonstrate your engagement in it.

Figure 53: Do's and don'ts during a press interview

- Refer to important facts as frequently as you can.

- Cut back on interruptions. Lend somebody else your smartphone and beeper, or switch it off.

- Look the reporter in the eye. Do not glance at the cam if the journalist is there. Maintaining eye contact is essential for conveying a strong and upbeat attitude. Gazing down could let you appear unresponsive while glancing at the outside can give the impression that you are being evasive or shifty.

- When answering a query, avoid repeating a negative remark made by the interviewer. Constantly use a positive tone when responding.

- Steer clear of abbreviations, business lingo, and jargon. The people are receiving the facts you provide through journalists. It is crucial to choose the language that everybody can comprehend.

- Do not ever guess. It is natural to do your hardest to think of a response, but being overconfident in a press interview could damage the image of your company. If you are not sure, admit it and commit to giving your finest to learn the solution and return to them.

- Be accommodating, but never lose sight of your goal. You are not there to simply respond to the interviewer's queries; rather, one is there to make your main points known. One must constantly work your signals in, even if you shouldn't be evasive.

Seminars

A seminar comprises a discourse where the findings of an in-depth study or research are delivered orally or in documented papers. The primary goals of a seminar are to exchange information and hear the opinions of others with similar levels of expertise. Typically, the main research is presented by one speaker, and then that work is thoroughly discussed. The audience members converse with the presenter and offer their opinions on what they heard.

- A seminar is typically a type of intellectual contact that is provided by an institution or by a business or professional group.

- It serves the purpose of convening smaller teams for regular sessions that each focus on a different topic and require active participation from all attendees.

- A relatively official presentation of the study or an extended conversation with the seminar presenter or faculty are two common ways to do this.

- To ensure that things are finished on schedule, create a timeframe for organizing your seminar starting from the date of the event.

- Typically, attendees should have some background in the topic being discussed. The purpose of the seminar approach is to familiarise learners with the technique of their selected field in greater detail and to provide them the opportunity to communicate with instances of real-world issues that are constantly encountered during the study.

- Fundamentally, it serves as a forum for discussion, question-asking, and debate about the required texts.

- In comparison to the lecture-based approach of professional instruction, it is comparatively informal.

Workshop

A meeting or educational session that lasts for days is referred to as a workshop. In speaking, it is more work-focused, with all group members participating and being guided by specialized asset people. It stresses problem-solving, practical instruction, and participant participation. When there is a real demo present, a symposium, presentation, or conference frequently turns into a workshop.

1. Begin the workshop by wishing everyone a good time. Be "kind yet forceful" in your conduct. Display compassion, adaptability, enthusiasm, and a positive attitude.

2. Explain to members the session's subject and your intended workshop format.

3. Spend roughly 5 mins outlining the main challenges related to the workshop subject.

4. Encourage other group members to share their opinions on the topics being discussed to learn from the team's encounters. Pose queries of people who could connect their expertise to the questions being addressed instead of controlling the discussion.

5. Keep talking about the main concerns and sub-topics until everyone's attention is high.

6. Ask attendees for queries, and if they don't respond, start a dialogue by addressing specific members by their name (if possible).

7. Prevents one point of view from taking control of the conversation and maintains it on topic.

8. Guarantee that everyone has a fair amount of time to discuss the topics that are important to them.

9. Guarantee that the voluntary participation you designate makes details of the workshop's main themes. They can use this information to report at the session afterward.

10. Express gratitude to attendees for their involvement and focus at the meeting's conclusion.

Conference

A conference is a private meeting. A conference is typically a sizable meeting of people who come together to discuss a specific subject or to swap knowledge or expertise. A conference might well be conducted to share opinions on a challenge the company is facing or another topic linked to it, and it could even offer a remedy, yet the conference's recommendations are not legally enforceable. They resemble suggestions more than anything else. The attendees of the conference must enrolment to attend.

The salesperson might organize a weekly meeting of the salespeople for the purpose of reviewing the previous week's revenue and formulating a plan for the upcoming one based on their opinions. A conference might occasionally be conducted to teach new hires. These workers may attend a conference where the company's essential facts are conveyed to them, and through conversation in a casual setting, they are encouraged to understand everything about the company, its goals, policies, and so on. This type of conference could be categorized as an educational conference.

In the event, a significant business issue will take the lead and call a meeting to address issues of shared significance with representatives from other, smaller business issues. The host company chooses the conference location, arranges for the representatives' accommodations, creates a thorough schedule, invites notable figures to moderate different sessions, chooses the presenters, and after the conference transmits the documentation to major newspapers outlining a few of the conference's key points. These gatherings often last 2-3 days.

Etiquettes of business

Understanding which cutlery to employ at lunch with a customer is not the most crucial aspect of business etiquette. Regrettably, the ghost is in the minutiae as seen by others. Individuals could assume that you might not have the self-control required to be excellent at whatever you perform if you can't be relied upon to keep your cool in professional and social settings. The goal of etiquette is to represent oneself in a way that makes it clear you can be treated professionally. Being at ease in social situations is another aspect of etiquette

Figure 54: Importance of business etiquette

The success of both your business and yourself depends heavily on individuals. An unintended violation of manners has resulted in the loss of several potentially valuable and lucrative connections. The prosperity or downfall of a firm or an individual is greatly influenced by etiquette. Etiquette refers to a human's manners, sense of comfort, and ability to make others feel at ease. The secret to accomplishment is excellent business manners. To be successful in business, be respected by others, and sustain positive working connections with clients, customers, and workers, proper manners and etiquette are crucial.

When you consciously or inadvertently fail to exhibit proper manners, you are likely to encounter many challenges along the way to accomplishment. However, an individual would undoubtedly succeed in any activity if they are usually courteous and responsive to the requirements of people who perform for them by abiding by the fundamentals of etiquette.

Making a profit is simpler than gaining the admiration and respect of those who recognize and work with you, such as co-workers and workers. If you adhere to the accompanying corporate etiquette advice, your life would be much simpler:

- Greet everyone you deal with respectfully, regardless of their status within the company, and make it a point to always be friendly, no matter what.

- To renew your recollection about the individuals you're anticipated to encounter at a gathering, use your contact list or "individuals database."

- Express regret when someone is offended.

- Expressing your gratitude to others will uplift their spirits and enhance productivity.

- Maintain track of the individuals who are important to you, congratulate them when they get a raise, and send them wishes on their birthdays, anniversaries, and other events.

- When holding a conference, ensure that everyone is aware of the agenda, the meeting's goal, the topics up for discussion, and the anticipated session length.

- It is common politeness to distribute meeting minutes and conclusions and to express gratitude to each member following the session.

- If you are not able to respond to a call, leave a courteous note on the voice mail, and someone will contact you back as soon as possible. When someone is on the line, never be abrupt or irritated.

- Regardless of whether they are an employee, client, or etiquette of a business acquaintance, never leave someone waiting. Never arrive late for a conference or the job.

- Attire is another crucial component of upholding proper business etiquette. Tycoons must have impeccable grooming. To avoid giving their co-workers a false perception, women must dress properly. Take the necessary precautions to avoid causing yourself a lot of shame.

- To maintain a harmonious workplace, ensure that your staff members behave properly around clients and one another. A client will turn into a recurring one if they receive courteous treatment with a smile.

- The fork should be kept on your left. On the right side, place the knife and spoon. Your bread platter is on the left side because food is placed there.

- Cups for beverages, notably coffee, ought to be kept on the right side.

- When two individuals to your right and left have been served at a dining table, you are allowed to start eating. Invite others to begin serving if you have not been served yet the majority of your board has. Request a colleague to move other stuff so that you can just grasp for those in front of you.

- Do not express gratitude to your hosts after the dinner; instead, offer to the left and pass to the right. "Thank you" is viewed as a kind of compensation and is thus offensive.

Bibliography

1)   Abdin, M. D. (2008). The Barriers of Communication & Guidance of Effective Communication. *The Barriers of Communication & Guidance of Effective Communication (January 2008)*.

2)   Agarwal, M. (2007). *Business communication.* Krishna Prakashan Media.

3)   Al-Obaidani, K. (2015). *Ideological aspects of the translation of business annual reports in Oman (English-Arabic)* (Doctoral dissertation, Aston University).

4)   Akter, N. (2016). Employee training and employee development is the predictors of employee performance; A study on garments manufacturing sector in Bangladesh. *IOSR Journal of Business and Management, 18*(11), 48-57.

5)   Ali, M. O. (2009). Business Communication: Theory & Application.

6)   App, T. C., & Hub, T. C. A beginner's guide to business communication.

7)   Aswathappa, K., & Reddy, G. S. (2009). *Organisational behaviour* (Vol. 20). Mumbai: Himalaya Publishing House.

8)   Bahl, J. C., & Nagamia, S. M. (1974). Modern Business Correspondence and Minute Writing.

9)   Bardia, G. (2010). Smart Communication: The Key to Managing Your New Age Business. *IUP Journal of Soft Skills, 4*(4).

10) Benjamin, J. B., & McKerrow, R. E. (1994). *Business and professional communication: Concepts and practices.* Allyn & Bacon.

11) Bhatia, V. K., & Bremner, S. (2012). English for business communication. *Language teaching, 45*(4), 410-445.

12) Bond, A. (2007). *300+ successful Business Letters for all occasions.* Barron's Educational Series.

13) Bosticco, M. (1988). *Instant business letters.* Gower Publishing Company, Limited.

14) Bovée, C. L. (2008). *Business communication today.* Pearson Education India.

15) Bradbury, A. J. (2006). *Successful presentation skills* (Vol. 111). Kogan Page Publishers.

16) Bremner, S. (2010). Collaborative writing: Bridging the gap between the textbook and the workplace. *English for Specific Purposes, 29*(2), 121-132.

17) Bushee, B. J., Core, J. E., Guay, W., & Hamm, S. J. (2010). The role of the business press as an information intermediary. *Journal of accounting research, 48*(1), 1-19.

18) Carey, J. A. (Ed.). (2002). *Business letters for busy people: time saving, ready-to-use letters for any occasion.* Red Wheel/Weiser.

19) Candee, A. M. (1920). *Business letter writing.* Biddle Publishing Company.

20) Casady, M., & Wasson, L. (1994). Written communication skills of international business persons. *The Bulletin of the Association for Business Communication, 57*(4), 36-40.

21) Chaturvedi, P. D. (2011). *Business communication: Concepts, cases, and applications.* Pearson Education India.

22) Clark, C. (2008). The impact of entrepreneurs' oral 'pitch'presentation skills on business angels' initial screening investment decisions. *Venture capital, 10*(3), 257-279.

23) CL &Thill, B. JV (2014). Business Communication Today.

24) Cloke, M., & Wallace, R. (1969). *The modern business letter writer's manual.* Doubleday.

25) Cooper, L., Orrell, J., & Bowden, M. (2010). *Work integrated learning: A guide to effective practice.* Routledge.

26) Cosman, O. (2013). WRITTEN COMMUNICATION IN BUSINESS. *USV Annals of Economics & Public Administration, 13*(1).

27) Cruthers, A. (2020). *Business writing for everyone.* Kwantlen Polytechnic University.

28) Ćurlin, T., Pejić Bach, M., & Miloloža, I. (2020). Presentation skills of business and economics students: Cluster analysis. *Croatian Review of Economic, Business and Social Statistics, 6*(2), 27-42.

29) Duica, M. C., Florea, N. V., & Duica, A. (2016). Improving Verbal Communication from the Perspective of the Use of Organizational Voice and Silence. *Annals Of The University Dunarea De Jos Of Galati: Fascicle XVII, Medicine*, *22*(2), 118-124.

30) Fay, M., & Williams, L. (1993). Gender bias and the availability of business loans. *Journal of Business Venturing*, *8*(4), 363-376.

31) Flatley, M. E. (1982). A comparative analysis of the written communication of managers at various organizational levels in the private business sector. *The Journal of Business Communication (1973)*, *19*(3), 35-49.

32) Florea, N. V. (2014). Implementing a model of strategic communication to obtain organizational performance. *Land Forces Academy Review*, *19*(3), 256.

33) Gopal, N. (2009). *Business communication*. New Age International.

34) Guffey, M. E., & Loewy, D. (2014). *Business communication: Process and product*. Cengage Learning.

35) Guffey, M. E., & Loewy, D. (2015). *Essentials of business communication*. Cengage Learning.

36) Guffey, M. E., & Loewy, D. (2022). *Essentials of business communication*. Cengage Learning.

37) Halpern, J. W., Kilborn, J. M., & Lokke, A. M. (1988). *Business writing: Strategies and samples*. New York: Macmillan.

38) Hamilton, C. (2013). *Communicating for results: A guide for business and the professions*. Cengage Learning.

39) Hamilton, P. J. Process of Business Communication and barriers of Business Communication.

40) Harcourt, J., Krizan, A. C., & Merrier, P. (1991). *Business communication*. South-Western.

41) Hargie, O. (2021). *Skilled interpersonal communication: Research, theory and practice*. Routledge.

42) Himstreet, W. C., & Baty, W. M. (1981). *Business communications: Principles and methods*. Brooks/Cole.

43) Ibay, S. B., & Pa-alisbo, M. A. C. (2020). An Assessment of the Managerial Skills and Professional Development Needs of Private Catholic Secondary School

Administrators in Bangkok, Thailand. *World Journal of Education, 10*(1), 149-163.

44) JAYASREE, M., & RAGINI, G. COMMUNICATION SKILLS IN EMPLOYABILITY OPPORTUNITIES.

45) Katte, A. Y., & Joshi, A. D. (2019). Recent trends in business communication. *RECENt tRENdS iN ENgliSH, MARAtHi ANd HiNdi*, 74.

46) Kincaid, H. V., & Bright, M. (1957). Interviewing the business elite. *American Journal of Sociology, 63*(3), 304-311.

47) Kumar, R. (2010). *Basic business communication*. Excel Books India.

48) Kumbhar, V. M. (2013). Business communications. *SSRN Electronic Journal*.

49) Kyeyune, D., & Delilah, D. (2020). Answers to'Essentials of Business Communication'by Mary Ellen Guffey and Dana Loewy. *Available at SSRN 3621368*.

50) Lindsell-Roberts, S. (2004). *Strategic business letters and e-mail*. Houghton Mifflin Harcourt.

51) Mayfield, M., Mayfield, J., & Walker, R. (2020). Fundamental theories of business Communication. *Laying a Foundation for the Field*.

52) McBride, N. (2016). *Intervention research: a practical guide for developing evidence-based school prevention programmes*. springer.

53) McCarthy, G. (2010). Approaches to the postgraduate education of business coaches. *Australian Journal of Adult Learning, 50*(2), 323-357.

54) McLean, S. (2010). *Business communication for success*. Boston, MA: Flat World Knowledge.

55) Murdick, W. (1998). *The portable business writer*. Houghton Mifflin College Division.

56) Neuliep, J. W. Intercultural Communication. A contextual approach, (2003).

57) Nystrand, M. (1983). The role of context in written communication. *The Nottingham Linguistic Circular, 12*(1), 55-65.

58) Palmer, I., Dunford, R., & Buchanan, D. (2016). *EBOOK: Managing Organizational Change: A Multiple Perspectives Approach (ISE)*. McGraw Hill.

59) Polonskya, M. J., & Wallerb, D. S. (2004). Making oral presentations: Some practical guidelines and suggestions. *The Marketing Review*, 4(4), 431-444.

60) Prabavathi, R., & Nagasubramani, P. C. (2018). Effective oral and written communication. *Journal of Applied and Advanced Research*, 3(1), 29-32.

61) Ramachandran, K. K., Lakshmi, K. K., & Kumar, M. K. (2007). *Business Communication*. Macmillan.

62) Rao, P. S. (2008). *Management And Organisational Behaviour (text, Cases & Games)*. Himalaya Publishing House.

63) Rudansky-Kloppers, S. (2002). *Business Communication: In Perspective*. New Africa Books.

64) Schaub, M., & McClure, H. (2020). Flipping the Script: Students as Authors of an Open-Access Business Communication Textbook. *Engaging Students through Campus Libraries: High-Impact Learning Models*, 65.

65) Shitel, M. O., & Suprun, O. (2019). Effective business communication as a core element of business management.

66) Sigband, N. B. (1965). Other worlds to conquer. *Journal of Business Communication*, 2(2), 29-38.

67) Sova, D. B. (2002). *How to write articles for newspapers and magazines*. Arco.

68) Tambade, S. A. Recent Trends and Transitory Nature of Business Communication.

69) Taylor, S. (2004). *Model Business Letters, E-mails & Other Business Documents, 6/e*. Pearson Education India.

70) Taylor, T., Doherty, A., & McGraw, P. (2015). *Managing people in sport organizations: A strategic human resource management perspective*. Routledge.

71) Toth, C. (2013). Revisiting a genre: Teaching infographics in business and professional communication courses. *Business Communication Quarterly*, 76(4), 446-457.

72) Valentina, F. N., & Antoaneta, T. I. (2016). Improving communication with internal public and customers of an

industrial company: a major challenge along supply chain. In *Supply Chain Strategies and the Engineer-to-Order Approach* (pp. 17-42). IGI Global.

73) Wienbroer, D., Hughes, E., & Silverman, J. (2010). *Rules of thumb for business writers*. McGraw Hill Professional.

74) Young, P. H. (1994). *Electronic communication techniques*. Merrill.

✳✳✳